AN ANGEL TO
WATCH OVER ME

JOAN WESTER ANDERSON

AN ANGEL TO WATCH OVER ME

TRUE STORIES OF CHILDREN'S ENCOUNTERS WITH ANGELS

LOYOLAPRESS.
A JESUIT MINISTRY
Chicago

LOYOLAPRESS.
A JESUIT MINISTRY

3441 N. Ashland Avenue
Chicago, Illinois 60657
(800) 621-1008
www.loyolapress.com

Originally published by Random House (New York: Ballantine Books, 1994).

Scripture quotations are from the New Revised Standard Version Bible: Catholic Edition, copyright © 1989, 1993 National Council of the Churches of Christ in the United States of America. Used by permission. All rights reserved.

Art credit: The Crosiers/Gene Plaisted, OSC.

Library of Congress Cataloging-in-Publication Data
Anderson, Joan Wester.
 An angel to watch over me : true stories of children's encounters with angels / Joan Wester Anderson.
    p. cm.
 Originally published: New York : Ballantine Books, 1994.
 ISBN-13: 978-0-8294-3654-9
 ISBN-10: 0-8294-3654-5
1. Angels--Christianity. 2. Visions in children. 3. Christian children--Religious life. I. Title.
 BT966.2.A515 2012
 202'.15--dc22

                                                          2011046469

Printed in the United States of America
12 13 14 15 16 17 Versa 10 9 8 7 6 5 4 3 2 1

To my guardian angel.
Through the years, I have often lost sight of you.
But you have never forgotten me.

CONTENTS

CONTENTS

ANGELS AND CHILDREN

The parents were thrilled with their newborn, Jeffrey. They could hardly wait to introduce him to his big brother, three-year-old Mike. "Mikey, you'll be a big help," Mommy told him when she brought Jeffrey home. "You'll get a diaper for the baby, or pat him when he wants to burp."

Mike did not look very enthusiastic.

"Would you like to help me hold baby Jeffrey?" Mommy pressed on. She wanted the brothers to love each other, right from the start.

"Uh-uh." Mike shook his head and went to play with his trains.

This was worrisome. Didn't he like the baby? "Maybe he just needs some time to get used to everything," Daddy pointed out. "Let's keep asking him to help."

That's what they did, but as the days went by, nothing seemed to change. Finally, Mike showed a little interest in the baby, but it was the wrong kind. Mike announced that he wanted to be alone with the baby because he had something he wanted to ask him.

Alone with Jeffrey? Mike's parents looked at each other. The nursery could be a dangerous place for an infant, especially if his brother still hadn't demonstrated any affection! But it was a beginning, so they took all the lethal weapons out of the room, laid Jeffrey in a far corner of his crib, turned on the baby monitor, and hid behind the half-open door.

They listened as Mike walked across the hardwood floor. They watched as he reached the crib and put his little face between the bars. And then they heard him whisper:

"Jeffrey, tell me about heaven. I'm starting to forget."

Various versions of this story have been floating around for years. It's impossible to know the original details. But the important line at the end is always the same: "Tell me about heaven. I'm starting to forget."

Most children have a sense of the sacred, from their first days here on the earth. This makes sense, because young children have not yet built up the hurt, anger, and pain that we all experience to one degree or another. In the Christian view, children younger than the age of seven or eight have not committed serious sin so they have the capacity to know spiritual reality in ways that adults rarely do. We might say that young children have one foot in heaven and one on the earth, and for a little while they can be part of both worlds.

An alert adult will notice evidence of this other dimension—infants who seem to be staring at something that no one else can see, toddlers lifting their arms up to be held by an unknown someone, four- and five-year-olds playing very seriously with imaginary companions. Is it possible that sometimes those companions are not imaginary but the little ones' guardian angels?

Whatever mystical experiences children enjoy, they usually fade at about the time a child enters second or third grade, and many kids seem to expect it. "They [angels] go back to heaven when you're seven," one little girl explained matter-of-factly. Some kids mourn the loss, and others barely react. By the time children are nine or ten, most will have completely forgotten their early mystical experiences, as if a giant eraser had wiped everything away from their memories.

Seeing angels is really not as unusual as it seems. Traditionally, many of the world's religions recognize children's intrinsic awareness of, and connection with, the divine. The prophet Isaiah envisioned a welcome era in which warring factions would lay down their arms "with a little child to guide them" (Isaiah 11:6). Jesus cautioned against hindering children, "for to them belongs the kingdom of heaven" (Matthew 19:14). Some Native American and African tribal traditions are rich with stories that honor childhood visions and dreams.

After the early childhood years, children are finding their way in the world, and developing a devotion to angels isn't usually high on their interest list. However, if children hear interesting stories about angels, many respond positively (angels are a bit more acceptable to this age group than catechism lessons!). It's important to present information honestly without embellishing or slipping into legend and lore. According to Scripture and tradition, God made angels before creating the world. Judaism, Christianity, and Islam all accept the existence of angels to varying degrees. Angels occasionally take on human form, but they are spirits without bodies, creations that are different from saints. They have three main functions: to worship God, to act as messengers between heaven and earth, and to guard humankind. A 2008 Gallup poll found that three out of every four Americans believe in the existence of angels. Even more interesting, a growing number of Americans say that they have encountered angels; they have either seen or heard them, or they have sensed their nearness in some way. The largest group of believers, perhaps surprisingly, is those from the ages of eighteen to twenty-four years old.

In 1992, a wave of interest in angels swept through the United States, and more than 250 books about them were published over the two decades that have followed since then. My third book in what became a series on angels and miracles was titled *An Angel to Watch over Me*. It was originally published in 1996 specifically for children, so they could read it themselves and learn more about the heavenly hosts. The response to the book was splendid, and kids loved the idea that they could speak to these beautiful beings whenever they needed companionship or comfort. As I frequently explained back then, every happening was true (although in some cases, I could not interview the people directly) but we could never know for sure if each account was attributable to angels. Some might just have been coincidences. (Do you believe in coincidence? Neither do I.)

As the years passed, I learned that families often read these accounts together at the dinner table or at bedtime and enjoyed discussing them. Further, my readers continued to ask for books about angels that would be suitable for all age groups, not just for kids. I realized that I already had such a book. All it needed was some additional stories.

So here is a fresh version of *An Angel to Watch over Me*, including many different encounters with angels. It's still a book about children, but it's meant for anyone who loves angels. Use it to teach, to encourage, or to add a sense of wonder and possibility to the everyday lives we lead.

Oh, angels, keep telling us about God and heaven, so we don't forget.

NEVER ALONE

In the dream God's angel said to me, "Jacob!" and I replied,

"Here I am!"

—GENESIS 31:11

Five-year-old Carole was playing hide-and-seek with several
neighborhood children. It was a fine day in Missouri,
sunny with a light breeze. But Carole wasn't having much fun.
She was the youngest, and whoever was "it" always seemed to
find her first. It wasn't fair.

The next round of the game was beginning. Where could
Carole hide? Then she remembered the porch behind her
house. They'd never find her if she went under there.

The porch was raised slightly to allow access to a cistern,
an underground tank that holds rainwater. There was a fence
built almost against the porch, but Carole was so tiny that she

squeezed around it and crawled underneath. The tank was just in front of her. Carole had never really looked down into it. Because she had to stay there until someone found her, she thought it would be a good time to explore.

There was barely room under the porch for her to sit up, but she managed to drag the heavy lid off the cistern. Then, lying on her tummy, she looked inside. It was too dark to tell whether there was water down there. Carole inched farther for a better view—and tumbled over the edge!

She screamed as she hit bottom, at least six feet down. Fortunately, there had been very few storms lately, and the cistern was dry. She got up carefully. She didn't seem to be injured. But the hole was small, and what if there were spiders down there? "Help!" Carole yelled. "I'm stuck!"

Who would hear her, at the bottom of a hole under a porch? Although her eyes were becoming accustomed to the darkness, she could see practically nothing.

"Carole! Carole!" Her friends were shouting.

"Here I am!" she called back. "Here in the cistern!"

But everyone was too far away. Time passed, and Carole heard them again. She recognized her mother's and father's voices, along with those of the parents of her friends. "Carole! Carole! Where are you?" It seemed that everyone was looking for her.

"Here, under the porch!" she yelled again and again. But no one came. Carole had tried to be brave, but now she started to cry.

Then she sensed warmth around her, a reassuring presence. It felt as if someone were in the cistern with her, someone who knew how she felt. And that someone was telling her, without words, that everything was going to be just fine.

Carole's heart stopped pounding, and her tears dried on her cheeks. Who was it? She knew she was alone in the cistern—there wasn't room in there for another person—yet she felt wrapped in a blanket of consolation and love. *Will you get my daddy for me?* she asked the presence silently.

Soon, the presence answered.

Carole sat down slowly. She felt comforted. She would wait.

More time passed. Then, abruptly, Carole heard her father's voice, very close. "She's under here—I know she is!"

"Daddy, Daddy!" she called. "Here I am!"

Her father's head appeared at the top of the hole. "Carole! Thank God." His hands stretched towards her, reaching down to touch her fingertips. Was he going to fall in, too? But no. Carole stood on her tiptoes as high as she could. One more long reach, then he pulled her up, up, and into his arms. Dragging her out from under the porch, he sat with her in the back yard, as her mother and all the neighbors came running. Why, it was dark outside, and everyone had flashlights! "Oh, Carole." Daddy rocked her, and she could tell he was crying. "We've been looking for you for hours, combing the woods, going up and down the state highway."

For hours! It had seemed only minutes! "How did you find me?" she asked.

"We met here in the yard, to decide where to go next," Daddy said. "And then I felt a force inside me telling me to go and look past that little fence. I pulled it back and saw the open cistern under the porch. I never would have thought to look there, never in a thousand years, if I hadn't felt that . . ."

Carole laid her head on his shoulder. She knew. She had felt it, too.

"Mom, can I go outside and ride my bike?" asked Aaron, age seven.

"Well . . ." Aaron's mother, Wendy, looked at the clock. The family was leaving for the Wednesday evening church service in less than an hour, and she needed to get Aaron's little brother ready. "Will you stay right in front of the house and not get dirty?"

"Sure." Aaron slammed the door behind him and ran to get his black and red bike.

Wendy smiled. Aaron probably wouldn't stay clean. But it was far too beautiful a day for a boy to be stuck inside.

A half hour passed, and Wendy went to the door. "Aaron! It's almost time to go!" Aaron didn't answer. She looked up and down the street, but there was no sign of him.

Strange, Wendy thought. Perhaps he had gone to his best friend's house on the next block. Wendy decided they would pick him up on the way to church.

Aaron's grandmother drove up to pick up Aaron's family for church, and everyone got into her car. They went to Aaron's friend's house, but Aaron wasn't there. No one there had seen him all afternoon. "Let's ask the other children," Wendy suggested, frowning. This was not like Aaron at all.

Aaron's grandmother drove up and down several streets, but although many children were outside and everyone knew Aaron, no one had seen him. "Where could he be?" Wendy wondered aloud. She was now truly worried. They returned home, and she called her husband, Glenn, at work.

Glenn came home right away. By now several people had gathered in front of the house. "Let's all spread out and look," a neighbor suggested. Glenn and some of the men rang doorbells and inspected garages and yards. Someone else drove back to the neighborhood where the family used to live. Mothers put their babies in strollers and walked up and down the streets, calling out, "Aaron!" But Aaron had vanished.

Eventually, Wendy and Glenn phoned the police. Two officers came and took a report. Wendy tearfully described what her son looked like, what he had been wearing, and his black and red bike. She wished she were just having a bad dream. But this terrible afternoon—every parent's nightmare—was real. When the police left, Wendy turned to Glenn. "No one can help him now but God," she said. "I'm going to call the church and ask people to pray for his safe return."

"That's a good idea," Glenn said. He was trying to be brave, but Wendy knew he was as terrified as she was. She phoned the church, and the church secretary promised to ask everyone to pray for Aaron's safety. Then Wendy went outside again. Pacing back and forth, she looked at her watch. It was 6:20. Aaron had been gone for more than three hours! "God, please send help," she murmured.

Almost immediately Wendy saw two blonde girls, about eleven or twelve years of age, riding bicycles slowly down the sidewalk. As she walked toward them, they stopped, as if they had been coming to see her all along. "Girls," Wendy began. "I'm looking for a little boy—"

One of the girls nodded, as if she knew all about it. "He has red hair," she said, smiling.

"And a black and red bike," said the other.

Wendy felt a leap of hope inside of her. "You've seen him?"

"He's playing with some children in a backyard," the first girl said. "I have the phone number of the house there."

The phone number? Wendy could hardly believe it.

"Yes." The girl recited the number. She was smiling so sweetly at Wendy that she made Wendy relax a little.

"Glenn!" Wendy turned and ran into the house. "These girls know where Aaron is!"

Quickly, before she could forget, she dialed the telephone number.

"Why, yes," said the woman who answered. "There's a little boy in our backyard who matches that description. He's been here all afternoon." She gave Wendy her address, and Glenn immediately ran out to the car to get his son.

When his father arrived at the backyard, arms outstretched, Aaron was surprised that so many people had been looking for him. His friends had been elsewhere, so he had simply ridden his bike across several streets until, on the other side of the subdivision, he'd found some new kids to play with. Had two of them been blonde girls, about twelve? No. Aaron was sure there had been no such girls. Nor had he told any of the grownups there his name or where he lived.

Typical of Aaron, Wendy thought, and she didn't know whether to hug him or to punish him. And yet there was something odd about this whole episode.

How had the girls known where Aaron was or the phone number of the house? And how did they find Wendy? Even stranger was that, even though many people in Aaron's neighborhood had been out looking for him, flagging down passersby and stopping children to ask for information, no one remembered seeing the two girls.

Wendy never saw the girls again. But she knows who they were. At exactly 6:20, her church community had prayed for Aaron's safety. And just a moment later the little messengers appeared, bringing good news.

A Helping Hand

A torn jacket is soon mended; but hard words bruise the heart of a child.
—HENRY WADSWORTH LONGFELLOW

Three-year-old Joey was an active child. From morning to night, he ran, climbed, and jumped. Life was a glorious adventure—so much to see and do and explore!

Of course, it's difficult to keep such energetic children safe. Joey would act first and think later. But his mother, Susie, had rules, and most of the time her son did his best to obey them.

One Saturday morning Susie was running errands in the car with Joey strapped into his car seat behind her. As she drove down a particularly busy street, Susie noticed a sign for a garage sale with some colorful balloons bobbing around it.

"Oh, good!" She loved garage sales, so she pulled over and parked the car directly across the street from the sign. She waited until traffic had passed, then carefully opened the driver's side door, got out, closed the door, and came around to the sidewalk.

Leaning inside, Susie helped Joey out of his car seat and stood him on the sidewalk next to her. "Stay right here, honey."

Joey knew the rule about standing next to Mommy so he wouldn't get hurt or lost while she reached in to retrieve her purse. But there were so many exciting things to look at, especially those balloons, and before Susie realized it, Joey had darted around her and out into the street.

He was almost to the center line when Susie looked up. "Joey!" A truck was bearing down on him, coming too fast to stop in time. A woman across the street at the garage sale saw what was happening and screamed, too. Susie started to run.

But as she dashed into the street, she suddenly realized that Joey wasn't there any longer. Instead, he was standing back against her car, facing the traffic, his arms outstretched along the car's side as if he had been placed there. As if someone was shielding him.

How had this happened? Susie was too grateful to wonder. "Oh, Joey!" She ran to him and gathered him into her arms. "Don't you ever do that again!"

"Balloons!" Joey shouted joyfully, oblivious to the near miss.

After a few moments, Susie felt composed enough to walk across the street, clutching Joey's hand very tightly. As she approached the garage sale, the woman came toward her. "When I saw that truck coming, I screamed," she began.

Susie nodded. "I did, too."

"He's such a lucky little guy," the woman went on, looking down at Joey. "Imagine what would have happened if that man hadn't pushed him out of the way."

Susie stopped. "Man? What man?"

"He was older and very tall," the woman explained. "I assumed he was with you, because he grabbed your child from the middle of the street, swung him over to the side of your car, and stood in front of him."

"But what happened to the man?" Susie asked, astonished. "Where did he go?"

The woman looked around. "Why, I don't know. He was there, and then he wasn't."

Susie was getting a funny feeling in her stomach. She knew very well that she and Joey had been alone all day. And she hadn't seen any man nearby. Yet her busy little boy had ended up safely sheltered against the car.

"Each night I remind Joey to thank his guardian angel for keeping him safe," Susie says today. She asks for the same protection when she prays, too.

Veronica, a teacher in Utah, drove to school one fall morning down a straight road bordered by fields. Ahead of her on the road rumbled a white van. Farther down she could see several eleven- or twelve-year-old boys ready to cross the street to wait at the bus stop. "They had plenty of time," Veronica explains. "The van and I were far away from them."

Suddenly, a car zoomed past Veronica on the left side. Horrified, she realized that the boys were in the middle of the road up ahead. All but one had already passed the center line, but the last boy was slower than the others. He obviously knew he had enough time to cross in front of the van and Veronica. But his view of the speeding car to her left was blocked. It would hit him just as he passed the van.

"I felt so helpless—I was too far away to do anything," Veronica says, "or for him to even hear if I honked my horn." So she started to pray. What she saw next is hard for her to describe.

"It was as if an arm literally pushed the boy from behind. His back arched, his head was thrown back, and his feet seemed propelled forward by someone behind him."

In a second or two, the boy was safely on the sidewalk. As Veronica sped by, she saw him look back to see who had pushed him. "I will never forget the shocked expression on his face, as he realized that there was no one behind him."

At least, there was no one behind him he could see.

Six-year-old Eileen and her older sister Dawna were best friends, but they argued frequently. They were bickering now as they walked home from school together. "I'm going to tell on you!" Dawna stuck her tongue out at Eileen as the two approached a street they had both crossed hundreds of times before.

It was a busy street, and Eileen should have been more careful. But sometimes Dawna made her so mad! All she wanted to do was get away from her sister's teasing, so she darted ahead of Dawna, right into the middle of the street. Cars stopped in both directions, and Eileen heard brakes screeching. Dawna screamed, and Eileen looked back to see her sister looking at her, hands at her mouth and eyes wide with terror.

Just then Eileen felt a strong hand grab her by her collar, the fingers hard on her neck. And then she was flying, sailing through the air across the busy street. Thump! Eileen landed on the sidewalk. Dazed, she sat up.

People were running toward her, and Dawna was sobbing. Why were they all so excited? A car skidded to a stop next to her, and a young couple leaped out. "Are you all right?" asked the woman.

"I think so."

"Oh, Eileen!" Dawna knelt down beside her. "You got hit by a car!"

A car? "No, I didn't."

"You did," the man told her. "We all saw it. You were hit, and you flew through the air and landed here. The driver is stopped there, and the police are coming."

Eileen looked over at a car with a teenager inside, parked just behind her. The driver looked pale and shaken. "He didn't hit me," Eileen insisted.

No one would believe her. They had all seen the same thing: a collision and Eileen flying over the street and landing with a thud on the sidewalk. And yet, it was odd that the little girl didn't seem to be bruised or even the least bit shaken up.

If such a thing happened today, the paramedics would arrive and take any child involved in an accident to a hospital emergency room. But years ago, things were more casual. The young couple who stopped at the scene volunteered to drive the girls home, and the police followed them. Eileen's mother was terrified when everyone trooped into her living room. "Are you all right?" She hugged Eileen.

"I think you should take her to the hospital," one of the police officers suggested. "She doesn't seem to have any injuries, not even any bruises, but after all, she was just involved in an accident."

"But I wasn't, Mama," Eileen insisted. "A hand came out of the air and picked me up, and I flew to the sidewalk."

The police officer stopped talking. Eileen's mother stopped talking. Everyone looked at Eileen. "Perhaps you are a little excited, darling," her mother said carefully.

"Maybe a blow to the head," suggested the young woman.

Eileen stopped. Probably no one would believe her. But somewhere there was an angel who knew what had happened. That was all that mattered.

ON GUARD

Zack was born six weeks too soon and was so ill that he had to be airlifted to another hospital. There, instead of recovering, he came down with pneumonia. The doctors told his distraught parents that this latest complication was probably too much for the baby to overcome. They shouldn't get their hopes up.

Zack's parents, June and Kenneth, had prayed for a long time to have a child, and they fell in love with Zack the moment he was born. Now June spent every day watching her tiny newborn in the neonatal intensive care unit, his little chest concave as he struggled for each breath, his arms no thicker than his daddy's thumb. "God, God," she whispered. Her entire existence had turned into a prayer.

At the end of the first week, Zach was still hanging on to life. This impressed one of the pediatricians, who asked June and Kenneth if they would allow him to try a new medication with Zack. They gave their consent, and slowly, almost unbelievably, Zack began to improve. On the day they brought their son home from the hospital, June and Kenneth felt that they had witnessed a miracle.

But trouble set in almost immediately. Although Zack ate and slept well, he was still frail, and his parents worried about him all the time. Could he get pneumonia again or another illness? June especially found it difficult to sleep. She was always afraid that something might happen to Zack if she wasn't watching. She refused to even consider moving the baby and his crib to the nursery that they had decorated before he was born. "What if something happens?" she asked Kenneth over and over. Zack's frightening illness was taking the joy out of parenting.

One afternoon when Zack was about four months old, June put him in his crib for a nap. She was so tired that she decided to lie down on the big bed right next to him. She closed her eyes. It felt so good to relax.

Then she heard voices. A man and a woman were talking to each other. It sounded as if they were sitting on her front porch, just a room away. June couldn't understand every word, but they were definitely talking about Zack. They discussed how sick he had been, and they seemed very concerned about him.

The voices probably belonged to Zack's grandparents, who lived nearby and often popped in for a visit. Yawning, June got up, went to the front door, and opened it. But there was no one on the porch.

June looked in the yard and around the side of the house. "Mom!" she called. "Dad? Are you here?" There was no answer.

Had she been dreaming? The voices had sounded so real. Puzzled, June went back to bed.

As she lay there, she heard the same two people talking, again on the porch. This time June leaped off the bed, ran to the front door, and flung it open. Again, the porch was empty.

That evening, June didn't tell Kenneth about her experience. She thought the strain she was under might be making her imagine things. As the days passed, she continued to hover over Zack, worrying about his health, afraid that he wouldn't grow as other babies did.

One night, June and Kenneth were asleep and Zack was in his crib, still in his parents' room. June awoke suddenly. The room was dark, but she was able to see two figures peering over Zack's crib. As she watched, their outlines grew brighter. Each seemed to be wrapped in a foggy glow. June couldn't see them clearly, but it appeared that one was a man and the other a woman. Instead of being fearful, June was fascinated, even happy.

As she watched, the man reached in through the bars of the crib and gently patted Zack on the head. "Yes, there's Zack," he said, turning to the woman. "He seems to be doing fine now. Isn't that nice?" The man's voice sounded familiar to June. Then she realized it was the same voice she'd heard that day on the porch!

The figure of the woman nodded. Then she raised her hand, as if in blessing over the sleeping baby. Their images seemed to vaporize, and the room returned to darkness.

June lay awake for the rest of the night, wondering about what she had seen. When she told Kenneth about it the next morning, he smiled. "I didn't tell you before," he said, "but one evening when I was in bed, I saw lights over Zack's crib. They made me feel comforted somehow, as if angels were watching over our son."

Of course! June realized who the strangers had been. And from that point on, she and Kenneth stopped worrying about their little boy. "I don't know why these beings chose to visit Zack and to let us be aware of them," she says, "but we feel honored. Zack continues to thrive, and we thank God for his constant care."

Oh, yes—and Zack sleeps in his own room now.

Angels were obviously watching over Zack. But could he see them? Because babies and toddlers cannot communicate well, it's almost impossible for older people to know what may be happening in a baby's inner world. Infants "fresh from heaven" may still have the light of paradise in their eyes. Toddlers might assume that the figures they encounter are the norm. We should stay as connected with our little ones as possible, for they may have much to teach us.

Kathleen F. agrees. "When my daughter, Mary Kate, was almost three years old," Kathleen says, "I was tucking her into bed one night. We had just finished our prayers, and I began talking with her about angels." Kathleen had never brought up the topic before, nor had her daughter indicated any awareness of it. "I told her how much God loves her and that she is never alone, because she has a special angel who is with her all the time and who will never leave her."

Mary Kate responded immediately. "We have *two* angels, Mommy," she said, "not one."

Kathleen was a bit startled. Since when had Mary Kate become an authority on the heavenly hosts? "That could be," Kathleen acknowledged. "I know for sure that everyone has one angel, but maybe sometimes we have more."

Little Mary Kate was adamant. There were two angels for everyone. "Her conviction was so strong that I did not forget it," Kathleen says. "However, I did not mention it to her again."

Kathleen's fourth child, Jonathan, later had a similar response. He was about two and a half when Kathleen talked to him one day about Jesus and about how much Jesus loved him. "Jonathan was completely disinterested in the conversation until I asked if he knew that he had an angel who watched over him every day," Kathleen recalls. "Then he said, with an annoyed tone in his little voice, that of course everyone knew there were two angels."

Kathleen remembered the conversation she had had with her daughter about three years earlier, when Mary Kate was about the same age. This time Kathleen probed a little further by simply asking Jonathan whether he knew anything else about heaven. "He very matter-of-factly told me that God and Jesus looked exactly the same except God had silver hair and Jesus' was brown. Then he was done talking and wanted to play."

The kids were too young to remember these conversations, Kathleen says, but when they got older she told them about it. Mary Kate was very interested, and one Christmas Eve at a relative's house, she was looking at the Christmas tree with her little cousin, Thea, who was at the time about two and a half years old. Mary Kate noticed an angel ornament on the tree and remembered the story her mother had told her.

"Do you know what this ornament is?" Mary Kate asked little Thea.

"Uh-huh. It's an angel."

"Do you have a guardian angel?"

Thea answered, "I have two."

Three young children, three different times and situations—there are no answers here, just the same glorious story.

COMFORT FOR JOE

I saw Daddy taken out of the car. The angels set him down in the ditch.
—The Boy Who Came Back from Heaven: A Remarkable Account of
Miracles, Angels, and Life Beyond this World, by Kevin Malarkey

Joe and his family had recently moved to a new house. Joe missed his old bedroom, with its familiar wallpaper and the interesting shadows that the trees made on the ceiling. Maybe he would get used to things someday, but right now he was sad, a little confused, and very lonely.

What made things worse was that his parents and the older kids didn't seem to notice how he felt. Everyone was busy fixing up the new house and getting settled.

"Stay out of my stuff!" his brother would yell.

"Joe, I'm busy now. Go and play in the yard," his mother would say.

No one paid any attention to him.

One night, after Joe had gotten into a fight with his sister, his exasperated mother gave him a quick bath and put him to bed. Joe protested loudly. Although it was dark outside, he knew it was too early to go to sleep.

But his tired mother wouldn't relent. "You've been especially naughty today, Joe," she told him. "You'll just have to settle down." She closed the door with a little slam, plunging Joe's bedroom into darkness.

Joe cried angrily and even kicked the bedroom door a few times. It wasn't fair! Didn't they know that he was cranky because he felt lost in this large and unfamiliar place? His parents had promised to let him have a kitten when they moved to a bigger house. Now they were at the new place, but no one had said anything about a kitten.

All of a sudden, Joe felt something soft rubbing against his bare legs. There was a gray tabby on his bed, rubbing against him and purring in the nicest way. And—this was unbelievable!—there was another, smaller cat on his other side. She was black, with pretty green eyes that seemed to wink at him. Where had they come from, and how had they gotten into his room? Joe reached down and put his hand on the tabby. Her fur was like velvet, softer than the nicest plush toy he had ever owned. "Kitty, how did you get here?"

Then, although he had heard no sound, Joe sensed a presence. Standing in front of him was a chubby, gray-haired woman. She wore a flowered housedress and carried a large purse, as if she had just stopped by his room on her way to the store. She looked right at Joe, smiling in a way that made him feel loved.

Joe had never seen her before. But he could see her now, and he could see the cats, even though it was evening and there were no lights on in the room. It was as if daylight had come into the room along with his visitors, sending the darkness away. The cats continued to purr and rub against him. Then the lady came a step closer and picked him up. "It's all right, sweetheart," she murmured, patting his back. "Everything is going to be just fine."

The lady felt soft, and Joe relaxed against her, his arms around her, his head on her shoulder. Who was she? She seemed to know all about him, how sad and lonely he was, how much he longed to be understood and soothed. Joe sighed in contentment. All his fear seemed to evaporate in the shelter of her arms.

The lady rocked him for what seemed like a long time. Then she set him on the floor and let him play with the cats. Their purring filled the room, and Joe giggled as they jumped on and off his lap, their smooth tails caressing his cheeks. He felt peaceful, even happy. Everything would be all right. He knew it now for sure.

But his eyes were growing so heavy. He needed to close them for just a few moments.

Joe awakened in his bed early the next morning and looked around in wonder. Had his visitors been just a dream? But as the days passed, he felt strangely hopeful and calm. "I'm glad you are finally adjusting to our new house, Joe," his mother told him one day. "I don't know why, but you've been such a good boy lately that I think it's time to find you a kitten."

Joe knew why his behavior had changed, but he wouldn't tell. He liked having his very own secret, the knowledge that some special visitors were watching over him.

Although angels provide plenty of love, they aren't above teaching a lesson or two when the situation warrants it. Veronica, of San Antonio, Texas, willingly admits that when she was a teenager, her behavior problems affected her family. "We could never go out to dinner without some type of argument taking place. We bickered, we yelled, and the night was always ruined."

But one evening, the family had gone out for dinner as usual (you have to admire Veronica's parents, don't you?) but this time they didn't fight. "For what seemed like the first time, we enjoyed our meal, laughed, and shared stories of the day's events," Veronica recalls. "It was unreal for our household to actually enjoy an evening out." Nothing unusual had happened to cause the change, and yet everything had been so much fun! Veronica thought that maybe she could pay more attention to her own attitude.

The family pulled up to their driveway and got out of the car. "Look!" one of them shouted, and the others looked up.

"There was a brilliant blue ball of light dancing just above our one-story roof," Veronica remembers. "It was the prettiest thing I have ever seen. It was about the size of a big grapefruit, somewhat transparent, and a magnificent blue." Everyone saw it, and they were thunderstruck. What was it? And what was it doing bouncing over their driveway?

Then a feeling of love stole over Veronica. "Somehow I understood that God was happy with us because we didn't fight; we were a family, behaving the way a family should." The family stared at the dancing ball, watching as it finally vanished. The whole episode had probably only lasted a minute, but the kindness and awe it inspired have remained to this day.

When Veronica eventually discovered that angels often appear as balls of light, she considered whether the blue ball was an angel. But it doesn't really matter. "I know the Lord was smiling down on us that night," she says. "So when I find myself frustrated with a member of my family, I actively try to cool down and remind myself that God is watching, and I want to make God happy."

MIRACLE AT COKEVILLE

Children are the hands by which we take hold of heaven.
—HENRY WARD BEECHER, REVEREND AND SOCIAL ACTIVIST

Except for the families involved, the event at Cokeville, Wyoming, on May 16, 1986, probably slid into the archives of history rather quickly. Cokeville (population 550) was not even noted on some of the available maps at that time. The event itself received little to no national publicity then, and being rather close-knit, the ranching community wanted nothing more than to recover—both emotionally and physically—during the days and years that followed. Eventually, a movie was produced and at least three books written about what came to be called the Miracle at Cokeville. But that was years later. On the day itself, there was no warning at all.

In fact, it was a normal day for the 154 children attending kindergarten through fifth grade in this little hamlet. Everyone had finished lunch and was settling back into their classrooms. In the main hallway, a disheveled-looking woman announced that everyone had to gather in the first-grade room. Most children and faculty assumed it was for a fire drill, and others were hoping for a surprise birthday party as they walked obediently to the classroom without asking questions. (Keep in mind that this was nearly twenty years before the 9/11 terrorist attacks, and it was a small rural community.) But when they filed into the room, they saw a young man holding on to a shopping cart, a peculiar item inside it. Behind him, pistols and rifles lined the blackboard ledge. Something was very wrong.

The invader was David Young, who for five years had plotted revenge against the adults in Cokeville for firing him for misconduct as town marshal. Brilliant but mentally ill, Young had decided to hold hostage all the town's children and demand as ransom two million dollars for each child. He would promise to let the children go as their ransoms were paid, but in actuality he planned to blow everyone up, to a higher plane, where he would take his rightful place, he explained, as master of a new world.

During the preceding months, Young had learned how to make a bomb and how to detonate it. He had also talked three male friends, his wife, Doris, and his teenage daughter, Princess, into joining his revolt. The others knew only that Young was planning "something big" and as they met that morning, he finally revealed his plan. Rather than support him, however, the others flatly refused to get involved in this bizarre plot. Furious, Young handcuffed the men inside his van, then turned to Doris and Princess. "It's just us now," he announced, starting up the van and heading for Cokeville Elementary.

Throughout their marriage, Doris had been a willing servant to Young, and today was no different. She would carry out her assignment without question. Princess, however, couldn't believe what was happening. As the three silently parked, loaded up the material they needed and entered the school building, she turned pale.

Young began his reign of terror in the school secretary's office, where he presented a rambling manifesto and demanded a phone call from then-President Ronald Reagan;

parents would somehow have to raise the ransom. Trembling in the hallway and listening to the demands, Princess had had enough. "I can't believe you're doing this!" she screamed to her father.

"You're no longer my daughter!" her father shouted and threw the keys to the van at her. "Get out!"

Princess grabbed them—and didn't stop until she had reached City Hall.

Despite Princess's rebellion, Young had prepared well and was definitely in command. The teachers realized that the item in his shopping cart was a bomb; it reeked of gasoline and looked powerful enough to blow up the entire south wing of the building. The bomb was attached to Young by a string around his wrist and was sensitive enough that it would detonate with very little pressure. Doris was wandering the halls, rounding up stray children and faculty. In a few more moments, an entire generation of Cokeville children was imprisoned in the first-grade classroom.

Now Young explained the situation to the bewildered students. "You are hostages," he told them. "If your parents raise the ransoms, you will be set free."

"What's a hostage?" a first grader asked. When an older student attempted to explain, several children began to cry. The idea of a bomb was too terrifying to comprehend.

"Nothing bad will happen if you obey," Young told them. "But if you try to run away, I will shoot you."

"Do you realize what you're doing psychologically to these children?" the school principal intervened. "They'll be scarred for life." Young shrugged. But he did allow teachers to move their own students closer to them and to one another, and to open the windows, because several children felt nauseated from the gasoline fumes. Others were permitted to color, draw, and watch cartoons. The majority prayed, some out loud. Young didn't care. He had been a committed atheist for many years.

By now parents had heard what was happening and were streaming down the streets toward the school. A cordon of police officers kept them at bay, or else many might have stormed the school, inadvertently putting their children's safety at even greater risk.

Inside, however, something odd was happening. Nathan, a first grader, noticed it first: shining people holding hands and floating down from the ceiling, hovering over the children.

They're angels, he thought. They were smiling, and each child seemed to have his or her own angel. Then Nathan saw a lady who said she was his great-grandmother. "The bomb is going to go off soon," she told him. "You had better move over to the window." Nathan was bewildered but calm as he looked around. Young appeared to be leaving the room; he had handed the string of the bomb to his wife. The children moved closer to the window.

Two sisters, age seven and nine, had been coloring, but then they experienced a vision of their own. It was a family scene including a baby, and everyone seemed joyful and calm. Now the girls' older brother approached them, and they followed him immediately over to the windows, still holding their coloring books. Amy, a fifth grader, prayed with a teacher and then felt an overpowering sense of love. "I had never prayed before, but the words changed my attitude from despair to comfort," she says. "I knew everything would be OK."

Perhaps because of the growing awareness of heavenly visitors, the children became louder. Doris, attempting to quiet them, moved too quickly. There were two rapid booms, then the lights went out and a fireball raced through the room. The bomb had exploded! Children screamed as they ran for the exits and blown-out windows, many with their clothes on fire. As the children raced outside, adults ran to them and beat out the flames; then, after scanning little faces dark with smoke stains, hugged and held on to each child. "I didn't know so many people loved me," said one child much later as she remembered the scene.

Seventy-five children ended up with burns, and Young shot his wife, Doris, before he turned his gun on himself. But later, as the town sorted itself out and people realized that no one except the two perpetrators had died, the magnitude of the miracle took shape. Gradually, many children told their parents of the same occurrence, beautiful beings alongside them in the classroom. Some children said they recognized the beings from old family photographs. Others described groups of angels in white who calmed the children and told them what to do. When the explosion came, they were prepared. Even those who had serious burns seemed to recover far more quickly than expected.

More coincidences? Four of the bomb's five blasting caps never went off, despite being assembled correctly. A group of civil defense members happened to be in town that day and were able to give help immediately. And later, when officials eventually entered the classroom to begin the cleanup, many saw the outline of a white figure on the blackened wall—a figure with wings.

Cokeville was one of the first communities to experience a school shooting. Today campus buildings routinely include security systems, and students are told what to do in cases of attempted takeovers. Today, when human tragedies and nature's devastation seem to surround us, it is easy to feel abandoned, just as the parents in Cokeville probably did, standing helplessly in the school playground. But they learned that the story was not over yet.

Nor is it over for us. If we remember only one thing during days of fear and tragedy, it should be that God knows where we are.

The Cokeville story includes sightings of both angels and saints, saints being human beings who are now in paradise. There are many examples of saints appearing to people still on earth, and children often confirm our hope that our loved ones are safe in God's arms.

For example, Jessica was five or six years old when her beloved grandmother died. The two had been very close, and Jessica had often stayed overnight at Gram's house. On those special nights they would have a party, with whipped-cream cake and a red-cherry drink. Those happy days had ended.

"I was grieving as I fell asleep," Jessica, now a teenager, remembers. "But in the middle of the night I saw Gram sitting at the foot of my bed, her arms open to comfort me." As they had always done, the two played together, "and we had a party, with white whipped-cream cake and cherry drink." Jessica fell blissfully asleep, "knowing that no matter what happened, Gram would always be with me."

Could the little girl have simply been dreaming? Perhaps. And maybe angels left the red-cherry stains and smear of whipped cream that her father found on her sheets the next morning.

HAND IN HAND

See, I am sending an angel before you, to guard you on the way and bring you to the place I have prepared.
—EXODUS 23:20

Marie was driving on a deserted ten-mile stretch of red clay road to drop off her teenage daughter at a church-sponsored wilderness camp. She had been to the camp-grounds before, but this year the spring rains in Texas had been extensive, and the road was slippery with mud. In addition, her three young sons were bouncing around in the back-seat, and the noise was deafening. She loved her children dearly, but she wished for a vacation occasionally, especially from her daughter, Beth. Marie's mere existence seemed to be a problem for Beth, whose current communication seem lim-ited to eye rolling, sighs, and "Oh, Mother," whenever Marie attempted a conversation with her. Worse, Beth believed in nothing at the moment, unless she could see and hear it. So for now, Marie couldn't even share a faith life with her daughter. She hoped that in time Beth would grow out of this painful phase so that they could enjoy those cozy mother-daughter talks that were supposed to happen during these years.

Just then, the car skidded through an especially thick pile of mud. "Pray!" Marie heard the word in her heart just as the car slid off the road into a ditch and came to a stop, its wheels stuck in the clay.

"Oh, no!" Marie flung open her door and realized that the mud was almost up to the floorboard. There was no way they would be able to get out without help.

Marie could have panicked, but she decided to have faith instead. She turned to the three boys, who were completely silent, and said, "Sing your church songs—right now!—and don't stop until I tell you to, no matter what!" Beside her in the front seat, Beth rolled her eyes. Marie could have delivered a lecture, but at the moment she had to pray.

"God," she began, "please remember Psalm 91 and let the angels bear us up. If I ever needed help, it's now!" The boys, having finished a robust chorus of "What a Friend We Have in Jesus," continued to sing, and Marie felt peace spreading over all of them. Was it her imagination, or did the back of her small car lift up? In a minute she floored the accelerator and drove smoothly out of the ditch. "Boys, look back and see what an angel looks like!" she cried in delight.

"Momma, we can't see anything," the oldest told her.

"Well, it's enough that he is here for us."

"Oh, Mother-r-r," her skeptical daughter started, but Marie interrupted. "Don't say anything negative. Just sit there and observe."

The boys continued to sing, as they traveled on, with a brisk rendition of "Do, Lord." Marie was still praying. "Lord, I hate to bother you, but there's a cement road coming up. It goes over a creek, and the embankment is red clay," she reminded the One who had created the creek. "It drops off on each side, and I'm a little worried." Fear gripped her for a moment as they approached the trouble spot. "Sing louder, boys!"

Taking a deep breath, Marie sped down the crossing, gunned the engine, and shot up the embankment. It was the only way she knew to avoid getting stuck again. But instead, she lost control of the car. "We started to tip over the side," she says, "and then I heard a gentle tap on the back of the car, and it moved into the center of the road. It veered to another drop on the opposite side, and again it was tapped, and it straightened up."

The boys cheered, and Marie gave thanks as she made it across. She wondered how her stunned daughter was handling this awesome occurrence, but there would be time to talk about it all later.

In just a few minutes, Marie pulled the car safely into the camp parking lot, and she sighed with relief and opened her door. "Did we get us here, Mommy?" asked the youngest boy. "Did the angels hear our singing?"

"I'm sure everyone in Texas heard you," Marie told them. She could see that the mud had seeped all the way inside to her floorboards. Well, mud was easy to remove. She got out, went around to the trunk, and stopped in astonishment as the children gathered around her.

"Mom, look!" one of the boys pointed in awe. There on the back of the muddy car window was a large man's handprint.

Had the angels heard their singing? Marie had no doubt. And when she finally made it home safely, she was not surprised. "God does indeed give us a hand in our daily lives," she says, "and thank God for guardian angels."

PATIENCE, PLEASE

Each day of our lives we make deposits in the memory banks
of our children.
—CHARLES R. SWINDOLL, *THE STRONG FAMILY*

J ack could hardly wait for fourth grade to begin. Like other boys, he complained loudly about the loss of his summer freedom, but lots of fun things happened in fourth grade, and he was secretly looking forward to playing on the soccer team and changing classes.

About two weeks before school started, however, Jack developed a persistent cough and started to lose weight. He tried to hide his symptoms because he knew his mother would fuss over him. But one morning at the breakfast table, he put his head down on the table and almost fell asleep. With some alarm, his mother asked, "Jack, honey, what's wrong?"

Jack shrugged. "I'm trying to eat, Mom. But everything tastes like cardboard." He dragged his spoon through the cereal. Just the sight of it made him feel sick.

His mother got up and went to the phone. "I'm taking you to Dr. Smith's office today."

Dr. Smith, a family physician, had delivered Jack and his siblings and still cared for the family. He knew Jack's parents well, and when Jack's exam was over, Dr. Smith sent Jack out to the waiting room and brought Jack's parents into his office for a conference. Jack tried to eavesdrop but could hear only a phrase here and there. But what he heard was grim enough: "seriously ill," "time will tell," and even "I want you to be prepared." *Prepared for what?* he wondered.

Soon the office door opened, and his parents came out, looking tearful. The new drugs that could help people fight off serious illnesses such as cancer and heart disease were not available yet. The family was on their own.

Jack did attend school on the first day. But the short bus ride to school left him so exhausted that he fell asleep in class. "I think it might be better if Jack does his schoolwork at home for a few days," Jack's teacher suggested to Jack's mother, as both women attempted to be positive about what was a very serious situation.

Life at home was definitely different from what it had been the previous year. Frequently, when Jack's mother thought no one was listening, she allowed herself outbursts of tears. Jack's father came home early from work almost every day to sit on the couch and hold his son. Even Jack's big sister treated him like a king instead of a slave. No one actually sat down and explained things to Jack, but it was obvious that there was something seriously wrong with him, especially when the "few days" of home study turned into a month, and then another. Dr. Smith paid an occasional visit as well, but no remedies he suggested had any effect. Jack continued to grow gaunt, listless, and depressed.

One afternoon Jack was sitting in bed, quietly playing with a puzzle his father had bought home to amuse him, when he heard a voice over his left shoulder. "Mind if I sit down?"

Startled, Jack turned and saw a boy about his own age, holding Jack's favorite coloring book and Jack's box of crayons.

"Who are *you*?" Jack asked, a bit annoyed. Those were his favorite crayons.

"You can call me Robby," the boy said, as he sat down and started coloring in Jack's book.

"How did you get into my house?" Jack asked. Sometimes a friend or two from school would stop by, but Jack had never seen this visitor before.

"This is not your house," Robby said.

Now he was becoming annoying, and Jack was getting angry. "Well, I live here, and you don't."

"This room and this house belong to your parents, and you are just a guest here," Robby said, as he continued to color.

What an obnoxious kid! "Who are you?" Jack asked again. "Why are you here bothering me?"

Instead of answering, Robby picked up Jack's favorite toy, an airplane Jack's aunt had given him for his birthday, and ran around the room as if he was flying it. That was the last straw.

"Put down my toy!" Jack shouted. "Mom!"

Jack's mother rushed into the room, wearing her now-familiar look of despair. "What's wrong, honey?" She put her hand on Jack's forehead, checking for a fever.

"She doesn't see me," Robby said casually over his shoulder, as he loudly zoomed the plane from one area of the room to another.

Impossible! "Mom! Don't you see him?" Jack asked.

"See who, honey?" His mother was looking around in bewilderment, but it was clear she saw nothing unusual. Jack didn't want to frighten her (although he was becoming a little frightened himself). "It was nothing, Mom," he mumbled. "Nothing important."

Jack's mother kissed him on the cheek and left the room. Robby put the airplane back on the shelf and went to sit cross-legged at Jack's feet. The two sat in silence for what seemed like hours, just looking at each other. Jack began to feel calmer, although his head was spinning. *Who was this person, and why was he here?*

Finally, Robby spoke. "You and your family have been having a hard time, haven't you?" He seemed sympathetic now rather than belligerent.

Jack nodded, not trusting his voice. It was odd; he had been worrying about himself so much that he hadn't considered how worried about him his parents and siblings might be.

"I get mad sometimes because no one tells me anything," he admitted.

"They don't know why you are sick, and they're very frightened," Robby explained. "Wouldn't you be scared if they were sick?"

Robby was right. Everyone was part of the family, and what happened to one person had an impact on everyone else.

"You are going to get better," Robby continued, "but for now you are learning patience, and that is a very important thing."

"I am? I'm going to get better?" Jack didn't care if he had to be patient. If he could run and jump again someday, he would be the happiest boy in the world!

Robby was smiling. "Jack, when you go to bed at night, sometimes you forget to say your prayers, don't you?"

"I hardly ever forget," Jack protested.

"Well, I can remember a few nights when you missed them, but we won't go into that. What is the very last prayer that you say each night before you close your eyes?"

"That's easy!" Jack answered. "My angel prayer! Angel of God, my guardian dear, to whom God's love commits me here.

Ever this day be at my side, to love, to guard, to rule and guide. Amen."

The last few words caught inside his throat, as if a heavy object had struck him in the chest. The wind outside was whispering quite distinctly: *Angel. Guardian angel . . .* He looked at Robby. The boy no longer looked like an ordinary person. There was a glow about him, and when he smiled at Jack, the whole room seemed to sparkle. Somehow, without words, Jack understood that something special was happening and that he must learn whatever this beautiful being wanted to teach him.

Robby appeared to Jack frequently during the following year as he learned patience. Eventually, his illness went away, and he was able to resume a normal life. So far he hasn't figured out the reason for all of this, but someday he believes he will.

MY MINNIE

Now I lay me down to sleep,
I pray, dear Lord, my soul you'll keep.
May angels watch me through the night
And wake me with the morning light. Amen.
—TRADITIONAL ANGEL PRAYER

It was 1980 in Atlanta, Georgia, and Tabbatha was nine years old. The historical city was under siege that summer, she remembers, but not by an army. No, the person terrorizing neighborhoods, causing parents to look nervously over their shoulders and children to have nightmares, was a child murderer. More than twenty African American children and young adults would be killed before the man was found, convicted, and sent to jail. But during that summer, no one knew exactly how the situation would end. Everyone was afraid.

"I can remember the mayor on television, with a million dollars in cash sitting in front of him, offering a reward to anyone who could help capture this man," Tabbatha says. "Kids under sixteen had to be home by eight o'clock every night, and the police drove through the neighborhoods to enforce the curfew. Each week, our schools bombarded us with safety films and police officers teaching us to be wary of strangers."

Like everyone else, Tabbatha was nervous. But she was also very religious. "When I was little, my mother taught me to pray. I went to church every week. One Sunday when I was six and the preacher asked if anyone in the church wasn't saved, I got up and went to the front, to accept Jesus." Tabbatha's mother wondered whether her little daughter knew what she was doing. But Tabbatha knew. "Later a youth minister told us we could pray for anything, at any time, and I did."

At times Tabbatha felt a female presence around her, as if someone special were watching her. Occasionally, the presence seemed to speak to her, and Tabbatha would answer, inside her head. "I told her about my fears as well as fun things," she says, "and she would tell me 'Don't go here,' or

'Don't do this.' I named her Minnie and figured she must be my guardian angel."

When Tabbatha was seven, she had awakened one night to see a figure in the doorway. "At first I was scared, but then I realized it was Minnie, and I was actually seeing her for the first time," she says. "We talked—the whole conversation happened inside my mind—and Minnie told me that she wouldn't be talking to me anymore, but she would always be watching me."

And so, two years later, as that fearful summer progressed, Tabbatha worried about her safety, just as all Atlanta children did. But somewhere deep within was a little extra confidence. She felt that Minnie was nearby.

One afternoon Tabbatha was in her front yard playing football with her friends, Amanda and Michael. Michael decided to go home, and the girls decided to climb a tree, then roll around lazily on the grass.

Soon a large pea-green car pulled up alongside them, and the driver looked out. "I've got some cute puppies to find homes for, girls," he said. "Want to see them?"

Puppies! Of course they wanted a peek. Both children started toward the car, and then Tabbatha paused. Something just didn't seem right. And hadn't grown-ups been telling them to be cautious about strangers?

"I don't think—" she began, then stopped in surprise. Despite all the warnings, Amanda was trotting right up to the car. "Amanda, stop!" Tabbatha shouted. Then, horrified, she watched the man suddenly reach through the open window and grab Amanda.

"Help!" Both girls began to scream. Tabbatha ran and caught Amanda around her waist, trying to drag her out of the man's grasp. She wouldn't let her friend be taken away, she wouldn't! Grimly, she hung on, still screaming. But no one came outside to help, and the man wouldn't let go! Tabbatha pulled Amanda with every ounce of strength she had, but she could feel both of them losing ground, being lifted farther up through the window. They were going to end up like all those kids on the news! "God, send help!" Tabbatha cried out loud. "We don't want to die!"

By now, Amanda was almost completely inside the car, and Tabbatha's waist was level with the window, her feet barely touching the ground. Suddenly, she felt someone's arms going around her waist. Whoever it was, was pulling her hard from behind, and she felt as though she would split in two! Then both girls went flying backward, several feet above the street, and landed on the grass. With its tires squealing, the car sped away.

The girls jumped to their feet, crying loudly, and Tabbatha looked around. Had Michael come back and rescued them? No, he would have been too small to pull the two of them away from that strong, insistent man. So who had? Shocked, she realized that there was no one there. They were all alone.

Tabbatha's mother wept when she heard what had happened. "Thank God you're safe!" she kept saying, as she hugged Tabbatha and wiped her eyes. "Thank God!"

And thank Minnie, too, Tabbatha thought. She had always wondered whether her angel was still nearby. Now she knew for sure.

LADY IN THE LIGHT

You have a lifetime to work, but children are only young once.
—POLISH PROVERB

It was Friday, and six-year-old Dale walked home from school alone. Although his family had just moved to their new house near Columbus, Ohio, Dale already knew the route to school. He loved being in first grade, being one of the big kids like his older sister. Every morning he waved good-bye to his baby brother, who had to stay home with Mom, and looked forward to showing his teacher, Mrs. Sherman, how well he was learning to read and write.

Dale was also happy because it was end of the week, and he'd spend a lot of time tomorrow with his dad. Dale's father was an engineer for a company in Columbus, but he was also a pilot in the Air Force Reserve. Every few weeks, Dad packed his suitcase, hugged Mom and the kids, and left to spend a weekend flying. "Pilots have to be ready for anything," he once told Dale. "So every now and then, we practice."

"Where do you fly when you're in the plane?" Dale had asked.

"Oh, lots of places," Dad had explained. "But I always come home in a day or two, Dale. Remember that, in case you start to miss me."

The coming weekend wasn't one of Dad's flying times. Dale knew it because this morning they had made plans to go fishing on Saturday. Dale smiled. Weekends with Dad around were the most fun of all.

He raced into the kitchen. "I'm home, Mom!" he called, putting his papers on the counter for her to see. His teacher, Mrs. Sherman, had put silver stars on them, and Mom would hang them on the refrigerator. His dad wasn't home yet, but that was OK. He'd be here for dinner tonight, and tomorrow morning they would go fishing together.

But Dad didn't come home for dinner. Mom got more and more worried, but when she finally phoned the place where he worked, it was closed. No one answered. *So where had Dad gone?* Dale wondered. *And why hadn't he phoned?* Finally, it was time for bed, and Dale began to cry. "I want to see Dad," he told his mother.

"Don't worry, Dale. I'm sure he's fine. He'll be home soon." Mom tried to comfort him, but she looked scared, and Dale felt the same way. Dad had never gone away like this before without telling anyone. Dale felt like his world was turning upside down.

The following morning, however, Dale awakened to see his mother at his bedroom door, a smile on her face.

"Is Dad home?" Dale asked, jumping out of bed.

"No, honey." Mom came and put her arm around him. "Last night Dad got called by the Air Force Reserve. He had to fly to Egypt right away. Do you know where Egypt is?"

Dale shook his head.

"It's very far," his mother said. "We'll look it up on a map later."

"Will he be home today?"

"No. He won't be home for a while."

"How long?"

"I don't know. But when the Air Force calls their reserve pilots to active duty, they just have to go."

Dale frowned. The whole thing sounded strange. But he guessed there was nothing he could do about it. When Dad came home, he'd explain.

But Dad didn't come home. Days turned into weeks. A month went by, and still no Dad. Dale's mother received several reports from the Air Force, which she shared with the children. But Dale was getting a funny feeling in his stomach. *Hadn't Dad told him that he would always come home in a day or two? Then why was he gone so long this time? What if those reports were just a trick, to keep the family from finding out that Dad was never coming back! Maybe he had left them. Maybe . . .* Dale's stomach felt sick now. *Maybe Dad was dead.*

Dale grew quieter. He ate very little and barely spoke at home. He wouldn't read out loud anymore in school, and he never raised his hand. "Dale seems to be grieving," he heard Mrs. Sherman tell his mother one day. "What has happened to him?"

"I'm not sure exactly," his mother answered. "Dale misses his father. But he won't talk to me about why he's so sad." Dale realized that Mom didn't know Dad had died. And he wasn't going to be the one to tell her.

Later Mom brought Dale to the doctor, and Dale heard them talking about something called depression. The doctor sat next to Dale and held his hand. "Your Dad is just away on a job for the Air Force," he said. "You understand that, don't you?"

Dale wouldn't answer. He was angry at Dad for dying, angry that the others pretended not to know. But if he talked about it, he would start to cry, and then Mom would know about Dad, and she would start to cry. So he wouldn't say a word.

Dale's father had been gone for more than a month when Dale went to bed one night. He lay in the darkness with that familiar hurt, sick feeling in his stomach. Was he ever going to see his dad again? Maybe if Dale asked God, God would let him go to Dad.

Just then, Dale saw something glowing in the corner of his room. He sat straight up in bed. As he watched, the glow became larger and more radiant. Dale saw something in its center. It was a figure of a woman, but not just any woman. She looked like the pictures in a book he'd read about angels!

The lady moved closer to him, somehow bringing the light with her. She sat down on the side of the bed and took hold of his hand. Dale wasn't scared at all.

"Dale, listen to me," the lovely lady said. Her voice was like silver, all shimmery and beautiful. "Dale, you have been very worried about your dad, but you don't need to be afraid."

She knew his dad! "Where is he?" Dale asked.

"He's in Egypt, flying with the Air Force and helping the people there, just as your mother told you," the lady explained. "He had to go away suddenly, and there wasn't time for him to say good-bye to you."

Everyone had been telling the truth? His father was safe?

"Yes. I am watching over your father, Dale," the angel told him. "I'll make sure he comes home safely to you when his job is finished. You help your mother while you're waiting for him. All right?"

"Yes." Dale let out a sigh of joy, of peace so profound that he could hardly believe it. The sick, miserable feeling had gone from his stomach. He felt light and bouncy, and incredibly happy!

The bright figure was fading. Dale reached out for her. "Don't go." But then the room was dark. It was all over.

Dale's mother was relieved the next morning when her son leaped down the stairs and ate three bowls of cereal before running off to school. "Dale seems to be fine now," she told Mrs. Sherman when she phoned later in the day.

Mrs. Sherman agreed. "He read a whole story to the class today. I wonder what made him change?"

"I don't know, but I'm going to give God a very big thank-you for making my little boy well and happy again!"

Just a few weeks later, Dale's father came home, just as the angel had promised.

HOLY ORBS

*Bye, Mom. We love you! Have a good magic trip and don't forget to save
us front-row seats in heaven!*
—SEVEN-YEAR-OLD LISA, *FINAL GIFTS*

The loss of a child, no matter what age, is perhaps the most severe pain one can suffer, for in the natural order of things, children are not supposed to go to heaven before their parents do. Eileen was in the throes of grief. Her adult daughter, Kate, was dying of cancer, and Eileen was brokenhearted. Her time to say good-bye was growing shorter, and her own sorrow was making it almost impossible to be a help to Kate. If only she knew some special prayers or a way to make her daughter's suffering diminish. She would do anything for Kate, but what did Kate need?

Kate had an eight-year-old son, Johnny, and her illness had been hard on him as well. Now that Kate was home, receiving hospice care, visitors and friends were able to spend some extra time with him. One day a family member gave Johnny an old Instamatic camera.

Johnny was delighted. "He had never taken any photographs," Eileen says. "But he was a fast study and felt he could venture outside on his own to shoot the perfect picture."

Johnny was too excited to wait until family members came out into the yard to pose for him. Instead, he ran around, clicking at a tree here, a plant or bush there, shooting whatever struck his fancy. At one point he focused on the garden his mother had planted and tended during her twelve years of marriage. The last photo was of their side yard, near the neighbor's house. As Johnny took each photo, he set it aside. "Grandma, I'm finished!" he finally called to Eileen. "Come and see!"

Eileen was still in the house, sitting at Kate's side, but she came into the kitchen to watch as Johnny's little stack of photos lightened and developed. And as the images emerged, she could hardly believe what they were seeing.

"There were pictures of angels!" Eileen says. "They were in every shot, at least ten photos, superimposed on the original scenes. Johnny saw them right away, too—I didn't have to point them out to him." Could they have simply been shadows or scratches on the camera lens? How was that logical, when every photo was different?

One angel held a trumpet high, as is often seen in Christmas paintings—as if the angel were announcing Kate's return to the Lord. Other angels seemed to be posted at the front of the house, guarding it from all danger. There were angels in Kate's garden and others surrounding the side yard, a silent and serene barrier between this house and all the others.

"Mommy, look!" Johnny was so surprised and joyful that he ran to Kate's bedside and gave the pictures to her.

Kate looked at each photo and then began to cry, which distressed Eileen. Had the images frightened Kate?

No. "I feel as if the angels are here, waiting to take me to heaven," Kate told her mother. On her face was a mixture of sadness and peace as she gathered Johnny close to her.

Tears filled Eileen's eyes. She had wanted something special for her daughter, and God had heard her unspoken plea.

Throughout these coming difficult days, Kate would keep the angel presence stored in her heart.

Kate died soon afterward, but Johnny continues to keep the photos safe and cherishes them not only as a little miracle but as a sign that his mother is still near. "The distance from earth to heaven is only a heartbeat away," Eileen says. "There are angels among us. We know we will see our daughter again."

RESCUE IN THE SNOW

Silent move the feet of angels bright;
Unseen they pour blessing,
And joy without ceasing.

—WILLIAM BLAKE

When nine-year-old Buddy awakened on Saturday before dawn, there was more than a foot of snow on the ground. But he wasn't about to let a little bad weather keep him from a most important job. Buddy had just become an acolyte and was assigned to serve the 6 a.m. Mass that day.

When Buddy came downstairs, his mother was still in her bathrobe. "The roads haven't been plowed, honey," she said, peering out at the dark deserted street. "I can't drive you to church—we'd get stuck. Maybe you'd better stay home."

"No, Mom." A promise was a promise. "I can walk, honest. It'll be fun."

Buddy's mother looked doubtful. It was almost two miles to church. But their little Ohio town was peaceful and safe. What harm could possibly come to her son? It made her proud to see him taking his responsibilities so seriously. "Well, all right." She smiled. "Be sure to bundle up."

At first, because his route was downhill, breaking a path through the new snow was fun. Buddy hiked down the middle of Main Street in the darkness with no people or cars around. It was a winter wonderland, all quiet and clean.

But as he walked on, the drifts from the blowing snow seemed to grow higher and higher. His legs began to ache. He longed to reach the church so someone there would help him in and seat him near a heater to warm his quickly freezing fingers and toes.

Finally, Buddy arrived at the front of the church. He was dismayed to realize that the snow on the church steps was completely undisturbed. He must be the first one there.

The walk had taken longer than expected; shouldn't the priest or other parishioners have arrived by now? Using the side of his boot, Buddy pushed the snow aside until he could finally drag open the front door.

At last! He fell inside, then stared at the cold empty interior. By the light of the just-rising sun, he could see the clock above the door. It was already 6:15. He had been the only one to struggle through the snow. There would be no Mass today.

Buddy knelt in a back pew for a moment, where he began to notice just how worn out he was. His legs throbbed from pushing through the drifts, and he would have to do it all over again to get home. "God," Buddy murmured, "please help me get home."

The way home seemed endless, each step a struggle. For every little distance Buddy gained, he seemed to fall back even farther, pushed by the rising wind and his own exhaustion. Although it was daylight now, the streets were still empty; there was no one to ask for shelter or help. Buddy had to go uphill, and he looked with dread at the long distance remaining.

He wasn't going to make it. He knew that for sure. His legs had been pushing through almost waist-high snow for what felt like hours, and all he wanted to do was lie down, end this terrible journey, and close his eyes.

That's when he noticed that someone was behind him. A large man with kind eyes was smiling down at Buddy. Buddy was surprised that he hadn't heard the man's boots crunching through the snow as he'd walked up from behind. But there hadn't been a sound.

Buddy stared at the stranger. A woolen scarf hid most of his face, but oddly, Buddy felt no fear of him. The man said nothing. He simply picked Buddy up from behind, lifted him over his head, set Buddy on his shoulders, and began to walk.

How strong he was! And where had he come from? Buddy felt exhilarated yet peaceful, all at the same time. It seemed that he and the man were wrapped in warmth, an awesome connection that Buddy didn't want to break by asking questions. Yet he would have to tell the stranger where he lived. But as they approached the house, the stranger turned and walked right down Buddy's long front sidewalk. How had he known?

They reached the porch, and the man silently lowered his head and helped Buddy slide off his shoulders. "Thank you, sir." Buddy immediately turned around for a last view.

But there was no one behind him. No one at all. And although Buddy could see footprints up the sidewalk to where he stood, there were no tracks leading away from the porch. Buddy stood in astonishment, surveying the scene. His rescuer had gone as quietly as he'd arrived.

It took a while for Buddy to understand who the stranger was. He never saw the man again. "But I don't need to," Buddy says today. "I know he's still here, ready to help me again when I need him."

FIND IT!

Prayer is our most powerful weapon for change, and we must use it to protect ourselves every minute of every day.
—JOHN TESH

It was late October. The days were becoming cooler and shorter, and autumn leaves rattled as they blew across the streets of Lawrence, Massachusetts. Shortly after 6:30 p.m., as thirteen-year-old Patricia finished drying the supper dishes, the phone rang. Her older brother and sister were out, so Patricia's mother answered the phone. A few minutes later she came into the kitchen. "That was the doctor," she told Patricia. "He's calling the pharmacist and ordering a prescription for me." Patricia's mother had been bent over all week with a back problem. She had tried to ignore it, but the pain had become too great, and she needed some medicine.

Patricia's mother reached for her purse and brought out her last crumpled bill, a fifty. "You'll have to go to the drugstore," she told Patricia. "I know it's dark, but I need the medicine, and your dad won't be home from work until after the store closes."

Patricia drew back at the sight of the fifty-dollar bill. Handling money always made her nervous. Their family was not poor, but they needed every dollar, and Patricia hated being entrusted with such an important sum. But Mom had dark circles under her eyes, and there was no one else to get the medicine. Patricia reached for her coat. "The prescription may have a copay so please carry the change carefully," her mother added. Patricia needed no such warning. Of course she'd be careful!

Patricia ran the four blocks to the drugstore, dodging raindrops and hunching her shoulders against the increasingly strong wind. Mr. Clancy had her mother's medicine ready and had already rung it up on their charge account. "Put that fifty back in your pocket now, Patricia."

FIND IT!

"I will." Patricia paused at the store's exit and stuffed the fifty-dollar bill way down in a pocket of her jeans, one that didn't have any holes in it.

It was colder on the way home, and the rain came down harder than before. Patricia was breathless as she turned down her front walk. Her mother, who had been waiting at the window, quickly opened the door. "Here's the medicine." Patricia handed the bag to her. "Mr. Clancy put it on the charge, so here's the fifty dollars back." She plunged her hand deep into her jeans pocket and felt nothing at all.

How could the pocket be empty? Surprised, Patricia checked the other pocket, then her back pockets. Nothing. Her head started to spin. "I don't know what happened," she said, quickly searching her jacket. "The money's gone!"

Stricken, she looked up and saw doubt on her mother's face. "Don't you believe me? I lost it, Mom—honest, I did!"

"But how could you? If you put it in your pocket, how could it have fallen out?"

"If?" How could Mom accuse her of carelessness? Turning, Patricia raced out of the house. She would go back along her route and find the money.

Tears mingled with raindrops as she retraced her steps. One block, two—soon her pace slowed, and her heart sank. This was an impossible search. Darkness had fallen, and patches of fog made the path she had taken even dimmer. Gusty wind swirled damp leaves against her, and drizzle dripped down her collar. She would never find the lost money.

Then she remembered a story she had just read, about guardian angels. Were they real? Did they help people? Patricia was approaching the only streetlight on the block, its dim bulb hardly brightening her surroundings. "God," she prayed, "please send your angels to find the money for me. Please."

At that moment she heard a voice, not outside her head but inside. "Stop!" Too surprised to object, Patricia stopped.

"Look down."

Patricia looked down. She was next to the streetlight now, and right near the curb was a small mound of wet dead leaves. Patricia took a step toward the mound, then another step. She could hardly believe her eyes. Sitting on top of the leaves was a fifty-dollar bill.

It had to be her money. But on this wet and windy night, how could it have landed so precisely, in the only area with enough light for her to see it?

Patricia's mother was delighted to receive her money, and she apologized again and again for doubting Patricia. But Patricia was happy about something else. Sometimes life was hard, and she had to do scary things. But now she knew she'd never have to do them alone.

ANGEL OF MERCY

We shall find peace. We shall hear the angels, we shall see the sky sparkling with diamonds.
—ANTON CHEKHOV

Michelle grew up in Canada. When she had just turned six, she, her dad, and her uncle Jimmy had attended a family party at her grandmother's house. Michelle's mother had stayed home because she was expecting a new baby soon and wasn't feeling well.

The party was over, and it was very late. "Michelle, it's past your bedtime," Dad pointed out as they pulled away from Grandma's house. "Why don't you try to go to sleep?"

Jimmy was sitting up in front with Dad, so Michelle had the backseat to herself. She took her dad's advice, stretched out, and soon fell fast asleep. (This was before seatbelts were mandatory in Canada.)

There was little traffic, and Michelle's dad drove carefully. But as he approached an intersection, a car drove across it right through a red light.

The two cars crashed. All three were thrown out. Michelle's father landed first, and Jimmy fell on top of him. Michelle flew across both of them and landed nearby. But for some reason, she slept right through it!

Hearing the screech of brakes, people came running out of their houses, and someone called 9-1-1. Michelle awakened briefly in an ambulance. What had happened? She could hear sirens in the distance and the attendants talking to her.

"Michelle. Michelle, can you hear us?"

But Michelle was too sleepy to answer. She closed her eyes again, and everything went black.

There had been several accidents that night, so the hallways of the hospital were packed with stretchers. Someone laid Michelle on a cot in a corridor until a doctor could examine her, and someone else phoned Michelle's mother.

When Michelle finally did wake up, she was frightened to be there alone in a hospital corridor. Vaguely, she remembered an accident, the sound of a crash, and broken glass. Where were her dad and Jimmy? Had they been hurt? She started to cry. No one was taking care of her or answering her questions. Oh, how she wanted her mother!

Just then Michelle spied a little old lady in a shabby fur coat making her way down the corridor. "I'm looking for my grandson," Michelle heard her explain to one patient. The woman came closer to Michelle and then she stopped and looked down at her.

The lady looked like Michelle's great-grandmother, her favorite relative! Through her tears, Michelle could see that this was not really her great-grandmother. Somehow, though, the lady looked familiar. Whoever she was, the tender expression on her face put Michelle at ease.

The lady patted Michelle on the cheek and smiled at her. "You're going to be fine, little one," she said. "There's no need to be frightened."

Immediately, Michelle stopped crying. She closed her eyes for a minute, to feel the peace that had started to warm her inside. When she opened them, the old lady was gone.

"Michelle!" Her mother ran up to the cot. "Are you all right?"

"I think so," Michelle said. "The lady made me feel better."

"What lady?"

"That grandma in the old fur coat," Michelle said. "She was just here."

A strange look crossed her mother's face. "You must have been bumped on the head," she told Michelle gently. "I've been standing at the other end of the hallway for a while, waiting for permission to come to you. I could see you the entire time. And no one stopped at your cot. No old lady ever came down the corridor."

Michelle and Jimmy needed only a few stitches. Michelle's dad had worse injuries, but he recovered, too. Today, they wear their seatbelts whenever they get into a car.

No one at the hospital ever saw or identified Michelle's elderly visitor. But Michelle thinks she knows who the lady was.

WHEN THE WIND BLOWS

No one but Night, with tears on her dark face,
Watches beside me in this windy place.
—EDNA ST. VINCENT MILLAY

Twelve-year-old Garry was happy growing up in Texas, except for one thing. Every so often, rainstorms would come barreling across the open plains, bringing thunder, lightning, and sometimes tornadoes. Garry had always been frightened of wild weather, and whenever a storm came, he would start to cry. Although he wasn't a little kid anymore, his fear seemed to be getting worse instead of better.

One afternoon when Garry was alone at home, rain began to fall. Soon the gentle patter on the rooftop changed to hail. Garry turned on the television. "There's bad weather all around us," the forecaster advised. "Hail and high winds, even a few tornadoes in the area."

Tornadoes! Garry phoned his father. "Dad, please come and get me and take me to Mom. She's working at the store!" he pleaded.

"Calm down, Garry."

"Dad, please—I just want to be with Mom!" Garry blinked back tears as thunder crashed outside the window. His heart had started to pound frantically.

"I'll be right there, son."

Ten minutes later, his father drove up, and Garry scrambled into the seat. Dad pulled away from the house. "This will blow over soon," he said, trying to calm Garry. But the sky was almost black, and with each mile Garry became more terrified.

When they reached the store, Garry leaped out of the car and tore through the front door. Garry's mom was waiting on a customer, and she looked up, surprised. "Garry! What are you doing here?"

"Dad drove me," Garry gasped. "Mom, there's a tornado coming!"

"Honey, you're white as a sheet! I'm sure it's going to be fine. Let's go check it out just to be sure." Quickly, his mother and the other customers went outside.

Garry followed them to the door, then froze. Behind his mother, far off in the distance, he could see a funnel cloud! Blindly, he raced back through the store, pulled open the heavy door of the walk-in refrigerator, and threw himself inside on the floor. He knew his mother and the customers were right outside, but their nearness gave him no comfort. All he could do was lie there in the cold darkness, trembling.

Then Garry sensed that he was not alone. There was something in the cooler with him, something warm and quiet and wonderful. Instead of terror, a feeling of peace began to flow through him. He could hear the thunder, the wind howling, but somehow it didn't matter anymore. Then a voice spoke to him. "Don't be afraid, Garry." It sounded like a man's voice, and it was the calmest, most loving sound he had ever heard. "There's no need to be afraid."

The words hung in the air: *No need to be afraid.*

From that moment, Garry completely lost his fear of storms. In fact, today when a tornado siren blows and Garry has to take cover, he doesn't mind at all. "I think the voice was my guardian angel, helping me get through my fear," he says. "I've never heard the voice again, but I'll never forget it."

Patricia's parents had gone out to shop for groceries right after dinner, leaving the twelve-year-old in charge of her four siblings. "But Mom, I can't keep an eye on *everyone!*" It was obvious, though, that Mom needed a change of scene. A strong thunderstorm had raged almost all night—no one had gotten much sleep—and everyone had been cranky and irritable all day. "I know you'll do a good job," Mom said as she all but dashed out the front door, with Dad trailing behind.

What was the good of getting older if all it brought was more responsibility? Reaching for the dish detergent, Patricia took a head count. All four kids were in the kitchen, bumping, teasing, and pushing one another. She had planned on making them help with the dinner cleanup, but playing outside seemed like a better idea.

"Stay in the yard," she told them, holding the back door open as they filed past. "It's going to be dark soon."

Dark, and getting colder, she noticed. The grass was still wet from the storm, and their beautiful double oak tree had lost a few branches. She took another head count and then started the dishes.

Patricia was working and half listening to her brothers teasing their youngest sister when a wash of cold goose bumps came over her. Startled, she looked around. What was that? Again came a cold chill, and then some words: *Bring the kids in. Bring the kids in, now.*

Another chill ran over her, almost like a signal. She had never experienced anything like this. It was an inner voice, but it also sounded as if it were right here in the kitchen. Was she losing her mind? The command continued although she tried to ignore it: *The kids. Make them leave the backyard, now!*

"Oh, all right!" she said to the empty kitchen. She had to shut off this mysterious message. But the kids would argue and yell if she made them come in. "Go around to the front of the house," she called to her brother.

"I don't want to!" he responded.

"Go!" Somehow she knew that time was running out. The kids knew that tone of voice, and dragging their feet, they walked toward the front gate.

At that moment they all heard a cracking sound, and then a sickening whoosh, and the earth seemed to shake. Patricia then watched one entire side of their massive oak tree collapse, almost in slow motion. It fell, covering the entire yard. Falling alongside the tree were electrical wires, sparking fire.

The kids! If they had been in the backyard just seconds ago, they would have been either crushed or electrocuted. Instead, all four stood in the front yard, staring at the scene. All four were safe—because of her.

Who had spoken to her with the words of warning? Patricia could only guess. But if this was what it felt like to be responsible—yes, almost an adult—she knew she could handle it, as long as an angel walked with her.

Visitors from Above

Music is well said to be the speech of angels.
—Thomas Carlyle

Nine-year-old Ashley's church youth group had been busy through December, rehearsing for the annual Christmas pageant. All the kids were involved in some way, either painting scenery or practicing songs and dances. There had been many late rehearsals and many missed meals. On the night of the performance, everyone was excited. "We all said a prayer backstage before the show began, asking God to help us perform well," Ashley recalls. The children could hear their parents and friends filling the church. The night was going to be special!

Being one of the younger kids, Ashley didn't have too big a role. When it was her turn, she and some of her friends walked down the center aisle, recited a few lines of poetry, and then sang a song with the choir, just as they had practiced. Soon their part was over, and Ashley went off the little stage. But she was puzzled. Where should she go to watch the rest of the pageant? She knew where her parents were sitting in the audience, but she didn't want to cause a distraction by climbing over people to reach them. Especially now, because there were some solos planned, and audience noise might make the performers nervous.

Ashley's church has a rear balcony that runs the width of the building. Right in the middle, there is a classroom, with a screen that lets people look down on the pews without being seen. Quietly, Ashley went down the side aisle to the back of the church and tiptoed upstairs. The classroom with its screened opening would be the perfect place to watch the rest of the program.

Ashley entered and stood still for a moment. The room was completely dark, because any lights would distract the children who were singing on stage. She had thought she was alone, but as her eyes got used to the dimness, she saw a figure kneeling on the pew under the screen. The figure was leaning forward, watching the musical performance with obvious interest.

"He (I think it was a he) was wearing a loose robe, which covered him completely while he knelt," she says. "And he had shoulder-length hair." The figure reminded Ashley of a picture of Jesus that hung in the church. But how could that be? No, it must be one of her friends, someone who'd also wanted a better view of the pageant. "Hi," Ashley said softly. "Who are you?"

Slowly, the figure turned around and looked at her. Ashley couldn't see his face at all, but she felt very calm and trusting. As she stood waiting for an answer, the figure simply faded away.

Impossible! Ashley went to the pew and peered under it. Nothing. She looked all around the darkened room. No one had passed her to leave. But no one was there any longer.

Ashley didn't tell any of her friends about what she saw, just her mom and dad. "But I wasn't at all afraid," she says. "I felt like I was honored. I thought it was neat that someone from heaven would come to watch our show."

Ashley saw her heavenly visitor only once. But Steven had a different experience. Steven learned to speak in complete sentences when he was very small, "which was fortunate," his mother says, "because one morning, when he was about eighteen months old, he had something special to tell us."

"A ball of light came through my window last night," Steven reported as he ate his cereal.

"A ball of light?" Steven's mother stopped buttering her toast and looked at him.

"Uh-huh. And it turned into a lady."

"Hmm." Perhaps Steven had just been having a dream, his mother thought. But he seemed so serious.

"The lady stayed and talked to me," Steven went on. "She showed me things."

"What things?" his mom asked.

Steven shrugged. "Can I have some toast?"

That was the end of the conversation that morning. But as the weeks passed, Steven continued to talk about his visitor.

She came frequently, though not every night, usually moving through his closed window in a large, round circle of light that illuminated the whole room. Steven began to draw pictures of her for his parents to see. The lady didn't have wings or a halo, but she was very beautiful. "Who is she?" Steven wondered.

"Ask her what her name is," his mother suggested.

Steven did. The lady's name, he reported, was Marigo. She said she loved him and was an angel.

Steven was surprised that his parents could not see Marigo. One night his mother awakened. It seemed as if Steven had called her, although she hadn't actually heard his voice. "Was that Steven?" she asked her husband.

"No," Steven's father yawned sleepily. "You must have been dreaming."

Still, Steven's mother got up and tiptoed to her son's door. The room was quiet and dark, and Steven lay in bed with his eyes closed. She was about to turn away, when suddenly her son spoke to her. "Did you see her just now, Mommy?" he whispered. "It was Marigo."

"No, honey, I didn't."

Steven sat up, frowning and confused. "Am I asleep when I see her?" he asked.

Steven's mother didn't know what to say. She couldn't see Marigo at all, and none of her parenting books had covered this topic. But maybe some children could see things—wonderful things, heavenly things—that grown-ups couldn't.

Until Steven was almost four, Marigo visited him frequently. Then one day Steven told his parents that he wouldn't be seeing the angel again. "She told me everything I needed to know," he said. "What exactly was that?" his parents asked. Steven was not sure. "But I think I will remember when I'm supposed to."

Today Steven still misses Marigo and wishes he could see her. But he knows she is near. One afternoon when he and a friend were playing in a tree house twelve feet above the ground, Steven slipped and fell out of it. He landed on his face, but he didn't break his nose. In fact, there wasn't a bruise on him anywhere. "Maybe Marigo caught you," his mother suggested.

Steven smiled. "I think she did."

WHO'S THERE?

Vision is the art of seeing what is invisible to others.
—JONATHAN SWIFT

Monica, of Zionsville, Indiana, was excited when she and her husband found a townhouse to rent. It had lots of potential, but it needed a handyman's touch before the couple could move in. Because there didn't seem to be any handyman around, Monica got busy right away. She was scraping wallpaper off the second-floor bedroom one day when her sister-in-law, Connie, stopped by to bring some lunch. Connie also brought her two little boys, three-year-old Jimmy and eighteen-month-old Noah.

After lunch, Connie decided to stay and help with the work. "We closed doors to rooms with anything hazardous in them," Monica says. "Since it was a nice day, the screened bedroom window was open, so Connie pulled a large portable stereo in front of it."

The boys played well together, dancing to music from the stereo and staying in the middle of the floor, away from the wet walls. At one point Jimmy looked at Monica. "There's someone at the door," he said.

They hadn't heard a doorbell. Both women peered out of the second-floor window, which overlooked a little deck and courtyard littered with debris. Monica called down, but no one answered, so she resumed her work. A few minutes later, Jimmy repeated the message: "Someone's outside."

The women looked at each other. Was a prowler sneaking around downstairs, trying to get in? Connie went down to check. She looked outside, then checked the locked doors just in case. "There isn't anyone there, Jimmy," she told her three-year-old. But he was not satisfied. Several more times he pointed toward the window to the deck below and insisted that someone was there.

"Are you teasing us, Jimmy?" Monica asked, but she already knew he wasn't. When Jimmy teased, he always laughed. But he seemed confused, even frustrated, that no one would believe him. Monica went back to scraping, and Connie went into the bathroom.

Just as Connie reentered the bedroom, Noah climbed up onto the stereo. "Noah, stop!" Connie cried, racing across the room to him. But he had already reached the screen, and as he leaned on it, it gave way. The toddler plunged through the open window to the deck below.

Screaming, Connie raced down the stairs while Monica shakily dialed 9-1-1. Moments later, Connie ran back into the bedroom and grabbed the phone. "I'll give them directions. You've had some first aid—you look at Noah!" Monica wasn't going to argue.

"Noah was lying on the deck halfway on his stomach, and halfway on his left side," Monica recalls. "He wasn't moving, but I could hear him crying softly." Did he have a broken neck or back, a concussion, a broken shoulder, or internal injuries? "I don't remember ever praying so hard for anything in my life," Monica says. "I asked Noah's guardian angel to be with him and help him to be brave and protect him through whatever lay ahead." Jimmy came out, looking a little dazed, and sat beside Noah, folding his hands in prayer while Monica carefully began to assess Noah's injuries. No visible blood, and he could move all his limbs. These were hopeful signs. But of course, the impact had been hard, and who knew what the hospital tests would reveal? She could hear the sirens of the paramedics, and she again asked God and the angels to be near.

The paramedics arrived and carefully rolled Noah over to put a neck brace on him. *That's odd*, Monica thought. The deck was covered in bits of shingle grains that had rolled off the roof; her hands had little pieces of them stuck all over because she'd leaned on the deck to help Noah. But there wasn't anything on Noah's face, not a cut or scratch or bruise, not even the shingle bits.

Connie jumped into the ambulance, and it sped away. Monica looked down at Jimmy. "Don't worry, Aunt Monica," Jimmy said with the utmost confidence. "Noah's going to be fine."

"I hope so, honey."

Jimmy simply patted her. He had no doubt.

Just a few hours later, Noah came home, suffering from only a small scrape on his left arm. The scans had shown no physical damage, nor did he have any emotional reaction to what had happened; he was his usual happy self. The extended family, who had gathered to give thanks, looked at one another. How could this be? How had this vulnerable toddler escaped serious injury?

Jimmy had the answer. "Someone caught Noah," he said quietly. "Someone outside."

Tingles went up Monica's spine. She thought of the day, of Jimmy's constant insistence that someone was nearby, someone that none of them could see. But she understood. Noah's angel had been there to break his fall, and Jimmy had seen him waiting.

"Jimmy is not the type to make up such a thing," Monica says today. "Nor had any of us taught him about angels." But she believes that God performs miracles for us all on a daily basis. And she will never forget this one.

STEERING CLEAR

Make yourself familiar with the angels and behold them frequently in spirit; for without being seen, they are present with you.
—St. Francis de Sales

When Beth's mother went to visit a friend, she took along five-year-old Beth and Beth's two little sisters. The girls played in the big backyard all afternoon, until it was time to go home.

Their car was parked in front of the house, pointed down a long, steep street that ended on the banks of a river. Their mother strapped Beth and three-year-old Meg into the back-seat and put baby Amy up front in her car seat. Then their mother got in behind the steering wheel. "Oh!" she exclaimed suddenly, "I forgot my coat. I'll be right back, girls." She slipped out the car door, closed it, and hurried back to the house.

A minute passed. Then another. Beth sighed. Mommy was probably saying good-bye to her friend again. Beth knew she wasn't supposed to get out from under the seat strap, but sometimes grown-ups talked for so long. She and Meg wiggled out and got down in the back floorboards to play with their dolls while they waited.

Another minute passed, and then Beth felt the car move forward. Had her mother gotten back inside? She looked up, but she couldn't see the back of her mom's head or even hear the sound of the engine. Beth stood up. Horrified, she realized that the car was rolling down the hill, all by itself! Amy had somehow gotten out of her car seat, crawled across to the driver's seat, and shifted the gears. Ahead of them, about fifty yards away, the street ended and the river began. They were headed directly for it!

"My babies!" Beth heard her mother scream behind them. Amy started to cry as the car picked up speed. Beth saw a neighbor, who had been cutting his lawn, run toward them, but the car was going too fast for him to reach it.

"Mommy! Mommy!" Beth cried. What if the car rolled into the lake? None of them knew how to swim. What should she do? What could she do?

Then, as she stood clutching the top of the backseat, Beth saw the steering wheel begin to turn very slowly to the right. There was no reason for it to turn like that; the street was quite straight and by now the car seemed to be traveling fast. But Beth watched the wheel turn farther and farther to the right, as if someone were steering the vehicle. Soon the car left the pavement and bumped along a grassy strip, moving slower and slower, and it rolled into a tree, which brought the car finally to a stop.

"Mommy!" Beth pushed against the heavy door.

"Oh, Beth!" Breathless, her mom and the neighbor reached her at the same time. Her mother pulled the back door open and gathered Beth into her arms while the man and the mother's friend got out Meg and Amy.

Beth's mother was crying as hard as Beth. "Thank you, God!" was all she could say as she hugged each daughter, amazed that they had not been hurt.

Despite the bump against the tree, none of the girls had sustained any injuries. In fact, as Beth later realized, even though baby Amy was no longer in her car seat, she hadn't bounced around at all. Only later did Beth tell her parents about the steering wheel and how it moved. "Do you think an angel was driving?" she asked.

Her parents didn't know what to say. But what other answer could there be?

Virginia also believes that angels occasionally take control of cars, when adults aren't being careful enough. "When I was in my twenties," she says, "I had three little girls, and one on the way. I had gone to visit my mother and stayed until midafternoon." By the time she decided to leave, the sky was darkening. Rain was definitely on the way.

Should she stay or go? This was to have been only a brief visit, so Virginia had few supplies with her, and she could be home via the country road within an hour. So she buckled up her daughters and set out. "It wasn't too bad in the beginning," she says. "Thunder, lightning, and a medium downpour." But as they drove, the sky got darker and the rain denser. Eventually, the downpour was so heavy that Virginia could not see the hood of her car! Terrified, she rolled the window down, trying to see the road, but she couldn't. Visibility was zero. She worried about getting hit by another driver.

Virginia knew vaguely where she was, and her fear deepened. There was nowhere to pull over, given the deep ditches along the road and the dense forest beyond. But worst of all, a railroad crossing was somewhere up ahead. "There was only a sign posted on the crossing, not a signal," she says, "because we were way out in the country." No one would be able to see the warning sign until they were upon it. And then it might be too late.

Virginia's daughters had fallen asleep. It would be too difficult to wake up all three and get them out of the car, in case they could somehow run to safety. Possible solutions flew through her mind as she continued to inch along the now-flooded road. She prayed for direction, for safety, for her unborn baby—and then suddenly the car chugged to a stop.

She hadn't touched the brake. Was the engine flooded? Then, to Virginia's utter amazement, the mist cleared for a moment. Just ahead of her was a train, moving quickly across her path.

Virginia sat for a moment, dazed, as the freight cars went by. It took some time for the train to pass, and when it did, she was able to see a little bit better. The storm was quieting down. Her family was safe. And her car started immediately.

"To this day I still believe that God sent his angel to be with us," Virginia says. "There is no way I would have stopped if not for the power of God."

GRANNY'S ANGEL

There is a destiny which makes us brothers,
None goes on his way alone;
All that we send into the lives of others
Comes back into our own.
—EDWIN MARKHAM

During the Great Depression, more than 25 percent of the population was unemployed. It was not unusual to see entire families homeless and without food, wandering aimlessly from one town to another, looking for jobs. People who had the necessities of life had a choice: keep everything for themselves or share what they had with those in need, even strangers.

Joan's grandmother lived along a highway during those days, and Joan cannot estimate the number of poor travelers her grandmother fed. "A lonely and hungry person moved Granny's compassionate heart," Joan recalls. And the aroma of fried chicken drifting through the air tantalized those down on their luck and led people to her door. Many offered to work for a meal, but Granny never required it. Helping those less fortunate was just part of her life.

"All the people who knocked on Granny's back door were men," Joan explains. "All but one, on a very special day."

When Joan was about ten years old, she opened the door one day to the most beautiful woman she had ever seen. Wearing high heels, a lovely pink suit, and a silk blouse with flowers and a ruffled collar, the lady was exquisite. "She even smelled good," Joan recalls. "I stood motionless, gazing in wonder." Where had this person come from? Surely she hadn't trudged down that highway.

"Go call your grandmother," the lady told Joan. Her voice was sweet, and she was smiling.

Still staring, Joan obeyed. "Granny!" she shouted, not moving an inch from the door. Granny hurried from the kitchen, wiping her hands on her apron. Like Joan, she was spellbound at the newcomer's appearance.

"I have no lodging for the night," the lady in pink explained. "Could you take me in?"

"Of course," Granny answered, already ushering her into the house. "Joan, go and catch a plump pullet for supper. Then you can snap the beans." The lady was staying! At their house! Joan was thrilled as she did her chores. And when she set the table with the Sunday dishes, Granny caught her eye and smiled. Both realized that something out of the ordinary was happening.

During supper the lady seemed at ease, but she didn't talk much. When Granny asked about her destination, the lady simply replied, "I have been given a charge to minister." After dinner, she retired to her room (where Granny had used the very best linens) and said goodnight. Joan remembers thinking that it was mysterious and lovely all at once.

Granny got up before daylight every day, and the next morning, Joan did, too. "I didn't want to miss a minute of being in the lady's company and smelling that wonderful scent." As soon as the bacon was ready, Granny sent Joan to their visitor's door to announce breakfast. Joan knocked gently, but there was no answer. She knocked a bit louder. The door slipped open, and Joan peeked inside.

Oh, no! The bed was made, and the lady had disappeared. But the sweet smell of her presence still lingered in the room.

"How did she leave without us hearing her?" a disappointed Joan asked her grandmother a few moments later. Granny's front and back doors had metal blinds attached only at the top, and whenever anyone came in or out, the blinds made a racket. Yet neither of them had heard a sound all night. "And when I answered the door yesterday, she told me to call my grandmother. How did she know about you?"

Granny had the answer. "An angel came to visit us last night," she said. "You never know when you entertain angels unaware!"

Joan believes that because her grandmother reached out to hungry people, God blessed her with an angel's presence that day, perhaps to encourage her in her ministry, perhaps to let her know that God was pleased.

Granny lived a long, full life, and just before she died, Joan sensed the presence of the beautiful lady again. "As Granny slipped away, an aroma filled the room, the same sweet fragrance I had smelled the day the lady knocked on our door," she says. For a while Joan sat there quietly, holding her grandmother's hand and feeling a majestic peace. Granny's angel had come again.

WHAT DID THEY SEE?

Grown men may learn from very little children for the hearts of little children are pure. Therefore, the Great Spirit may show to them many things which older people miss.

—BLACK ELK

Several years ago, Fred and Bunny and their two young sons visited a wooded and somewhat isolated site in central Ohio. It had been rumored that a young woman was having visions of the Blessed Virgin Mary there at regular intervals, and Fred and Bunny wanted to pray at the site. Yes, there seemed to be many seers bringing messages at the time, and it was easy to be misled or even duped by those who were not sent from God. Nor had the Catholic Church done an investigation at this site, at least not at that time.

WHAT DID THEY SEE?

But Fred and Bunny trusted that God would show them whether this was indeed holy ground. And their boys, who had never visited a shrine or done anything like this, might be inspired to get along better!

The family stayed at a farmhouse the day before the expected vision, and they recited the rosary with several other visitors. Seven-year-old Alex and six-year-old David were fidgety and restless throughout the prayers. "This is boooooring," Alex complained loudly, more than once.

"I want to go home," David added. Bunny felt like sinking through the floor. She wanted them to go home, too!

It had rained the day before, and as the family walked through the woods to the site, mosquitoes attacked them in clouds. Flushed and overheated, Alex and David raced around, chasing after a fawn that they had spotted behind a tree, shouting, pushing each other, and arguing.

As people knelt on the rough grass to pray, Bunny dragged the boys next to her, resisting the impulse to scream. This trip was becoming a nightmare.

But to her relief, as the seventy or so people there began to recite another rosary, David and Alex suddenly calmed down.

In fact, they didn't move for the next hour, except to stand up with everyone else when the visionary announced that Mary, the mother of Jesus, was in their presence. It was definitely a change from their behavior over the previous two days.

None of the assembly seemed to see anything unusual. No one pointed or shouted or acted as though something awesome were happening. Instead, when prayer time was over, families gathered and headed for their cars.

"Let's stop for something to eat on our way home," Fred suggested. "I'm starving."

"Let's," Bunny said. "I think I saw a restaurant sign on the way here."

Neither of the boys began their customary arguing over what to order. In fact, Bunny noticed that they were unusually docile; neither had spoken a word since the prayers had started. Maybe they would sleep on the long trek home.

Up ahead was a restaurant. Fred parked and everyone went inside. After the family had ordered, Alex broke the silence.

"Mom, how did they make the clouds open up like that?" he asked.

Bunny was startled. "What do you mean, Alex?"

"When the blue thing came down. How did it get through the clouds?"

Bunny and Fred looked at each other, both sensing the importance of the moment. "Can you tell us what the blue thing looked like?" Fred asked.

"It was the thing the lady was wearing on her head," Alex explained.

David looked up. "She had on a blue dress, too."

"But lighter," Alex added. "Lighter blue than the thing on her head." David nodded.

Were their sons telling the truth? Had they actually seen something—someone—on the hill? Fred decided to question them separately, before they had a chance to compare notes.

Over the following few days, Fred carefully quizzed the boys on the details of their experience, and they answered without hesitation or apparent concern and without conferring with each other. Both had apparently seen a lady at the site, and each described her clothes (including the "blue thing," a mantle on her head) and movements in much the same way and drew similar pictures. They had also seen angels; David's were little cherubs "with bright circles above their heads," whereas Alex saw five large spirits wearing colors "like a rainbow, only not as shiny." Neither boy had been at all afraid of the lady or the experience.

"At first I hesitated to believe it," Fred admits. "But now I have no doubt that the boys saw a vision. Maybe their slightly different views of angels was deliberate, so skeptics would not be able to say that they copied from each other."

Although it would be pleasant to report that Alex and David are perfectly behaved now, since they glimpsed the angelic realm, such is not the case. But they do regard their experience as something special. And their parents? "We have no idea why this happened," Fred says. "But we will regard it forever as a gift from heaven."

A Miracle for Isaac

Before I formed you in the womb I knew you.

—Jeremiah 1:5

It was an ordinary late-April day at the family farm in down-state Atkinson, Illinois. The five youngest cousins were enjoying playing together when suddenly there was an explosion in the barn, and a ball of fire roared through the barn door directly toward the children. As horrified adults ran toward the children, they saw that eight-year-old Isaac had received the worst of the flames. Isaac's dad scooped up his son, ran for the family car, and called 9-1-1 on the way. "The ambulance met them, and a second ambulance brought a burn specialist," Isaac's grandmother Mary says. "Help was there right away."

But once at the hospital, the grim reality set in. Isaac's burns were severe, second and third degree on his torso, face, and arms. He cried constantly from the pain (according to the Mayo Clinic, second-degree burns are the most painful). Within two days, the doctors at the local hospital transferred him to Loyola University's renowned burn unit in Chicago. The family later learned that burns don't mature for about seventy-two hours, and when Isaac's face began to swell, the local doctors were afraid that his lungs would swell also. He needed more specialized care, and it would be a long and painful process.

According to specialists at the Mayo Clinic, when the first layer of skin has been burned through and the second layer (dermis) also is burned, the injury is a second-degree burn. Blisters develop, and the skin takes on an intensely reddened, splotchy appearance. Second-degree burns produce severe pain and swelling. Because Isaac's face was covered extensively with second-degree burns, doctors wondered whether his eyes and ears had been permanently damaged. Isaac also had frightening flashbacks of the accident that kept him from sleeping.

Perhaps the worst part was the twice-daily two-hour scrubs, during which nurses remove dead skin to prevent scarring.

Despite some anesthesia, Isaac's pain was horrific. "Daga" (that's what he called his grandma), he later told Mary, "no kid should ever have this happen to him." Isaac has always known about angels, but during those first days, he wondered where his had gone.

When Mary heard the news, she got on her knees and cried out to God and to the archangel Raphael (patron of healing) to send an army of angels to help her grandson. "I asked specifically that Isaac's pain would be taken from him and given to me instead." But that didn't happen, and bulletins coming from the hospital seemed to be mainly bad news. Mary began alerting friends and passing her request to church communities. Isaac's maternal grandmother did the same. "Pray for Isaac," the message stated, as prayer groups, cell phones, and even the Internet carried the petition throughout the country: "Pray that he is free of pain. Pray, pray."

No one is exactly sure when things started to change, but less than a week after the accident, Isaac's appetite began to return. Because he needed protein, he became a fan of the Dairy Queen near the hospital, inhaling milk shakes whenever anyone brought one. He felt well enough to talk on the phone with his best buddy, who called daily and would do so until Isaac was completely OK.

His attitude was more upbeat, too, and his physicians felt that because his convalescence would be long and he would probably need skin grafts, he could go home and have nursing care there. Released so soon? "How could this be?" family members asked one another. Isaac still looked so damaged. But the little boy insisted that he could go home because he didn't have any pain. When Mary saw his burns, it seemed impossible for Isaac to go home. "His lips are blistered and raw; his entire face is raw," she e-mailed that day. "But he is in no pain. Oh, God, how great thou art!"

Isaac did go home, and nurses came in each day to remove the dressings and to peel away any dead skin. "They apply an antibiotic ointment over the entire area," Mary reported to her prayer warriors. "There is no more fever. They check everything for infection, and then they rewrap it and pull that pressure stocking over his head and face. From what I saw yesterday, it really looks good."

About a week later, Isaac's parents took him back to Loyola for a checkup. The surprised burn specialists had never seen anything like it. "Isaac, I wasn't expecting you to look like this at all," one said. "But you are almost healed! You don't have to see me anymore, unless some problem pops up."

Twenty-three days after the accident, Isaac went back to school full time, catching up on his missed days. He had missed his first communion ceremony but had received cards, letters, and gifts from all around the world, and was amazed and grateful (and he read every one). "No more flashbacks or nightmares of the fire," Mary says. "His eyes are fine. His nose is fine. His lips and ears are fine; it looks now just like a bad sunburn. The doctors say there will be minimal to no scarring, and no skin grafts are needed! And he is laughing and being the character Isaac has always been—all without pain."

Isaac did have a question for his grandmother. "Why can't I see the angels, Daga?" he asked her one day in the hospital.

Mary thought for a while. "Isaac, if the world could see angels, think of the traffic jams it might cause," she pointed out. "What would you think if you saw one hundred thousand angels in the sky or riding on the top of an ambulance, keeping you safe?"

Isaac understood. "I'd think God must be very busy ordering all his angels around," he said, smiling.

"Yes, God must be," Mary agreed. "And just think, God sent them just for you."

Mary still doesn't understand how Isaac recovered so quickly. But she says, "When your heart and mind are all scrambled with worry and helplessness, God says, 'Be still and know that I am God. Miracles will happen.'"

In Her Memory

Hush, my dear, lie still and slumber! Holy angels guard thy bed!
—Isaac Watts, "A Cradle Hymn"

Deirdre's family believes in the power of prayer. Deirdre, of Santa Rosa, California, was the fifth of ten children, with long curly brown hair, green eyes, and a gentle disposition. People were attracted to her beauty, says her mother, Patricia, "but it was her sweetness that held their hearts." The family was thrilled to have another daughter (they had seven sons), and Deirdre had many friends, a large extended family, a happy life in St. Eugene's Cathedral school, and even a sideline interest: Irish dancing.

It was an idyllic life, and then tragedy struck. "We were at her father's company picnic at Lake Sonoma," Patricia says. "She was swimming with her brother, sister, and cousin, and while trying to lift herself out of the water, she touched faulty wiring on the dock and was killed instantly." Deirdre was ten years old.

The entire school and parish of St. Eugene's rallied around the grief-stricken family. Food, care of the children, whatever was needed, they gave, and more than eight hundred people attended the funeral. Despite the prayers and kindnesses shown to the family, Patricia was devastated. She had just discovered that a new baby was on the way, and Deirdre would have been so delighted if she knew. Her daughters would never meet, at least not here on the earth. "We are Catholics, and we believe in the promise of eternity that Jesus grants to all who follow him, and we try to live accordingly," says Patricia. But grief can often overshadow faith. And then, of course, someone was legally liable for the faulty wiring, and perhaps the family would have to initiate a lawsuit. Patricia did not know how she was going to get through all of it.

On the Monday after the first Thanksgiving without Deirdre, the children had gone back to school; Patricia's husband, Marty, was at work; and the two preschoolers were still asleep. Patricia read the newspaper, waiting for the boys to awaken, and enjoyed the solitude. "At about 9 a.m. I sat back on the couch and put my feet up, thinking about the day ahead," she says. "When I closed my eyes, it was as if a tunnel opened and I was looking at my Deirdre. She was sitting on a beautiful, powerful white horse. I have never seen a horse like it before or since."

Deirdre was wearing a lavender gown, gathered at the neck, waist, and wrists, and she was barefoot. Her hair was in braids, and she had a great big smile on her face. Patricia could see little tendrils of hair that had escaped from her braids curling around her forehead. She could see her daughter's freckles and the small birthmark she had on her chin. Deirdre was healthy, happy, suntanned, and alive!

How could this be happening? It seemed so real, and yet the vision was inside her, not outside. Patricia also realized that it did not seem that Deirdre was aware of her mother but that Patricia was being permitted to look at her. "There was a child on the back of the horse with her, holding on to her waist," Patricia remembers. "There were children running along either side of the horse, too. Deirdre raised her right hand and tapped the horse to get it to go even faster." She didn't seem the least bit afraid.

For a moment, Patricia stole a glance at the surroundings. Tall grass, almost a golden shade, a perfectly blue sky, and a magnificent tree, a variety Patricia had never seen. She tried to look at the children who were with Deirdre, but their faces seemed blurry. Perhaps she was not to know their identities. Or perhaps they were angels?

As quickly as the tunnel had opened, it closed, and Patricia heard her little boys running down the stairs. Heart pounding, she opened her eyes. What had just happened to her? She called Marty at work and tried as best she could to describe what she had seen.

"I believe this vision was a gift from God because of all the prayers we received from family, friends, and even strangers who had heard about Deirdre," she says. "We chose to forgive those responsible for her death because it's what she would expect from us. We have tried to honor her memory by helping others in her name." There is much strength in prayers, our own and others. Patricia and Marty know they will see their child again.

HEAVENLY HOUSEKEEPERS

Let the angels assist you. They are always there to offer a shoulder or to help you carry your burden.

—JAYNE HOWARD

When eight-year-old Mehul's grandmother died, his family returned to India for her funeral. Mehul didn't know his grandmother very well, because she had never come to live with them in New York. But she often wrote him letters, and he enjoyed talking with her on his visits back to India. Now he would never see her again. The thought made him sad.

He looked around Grandmother's house. It would soon be filled with relatives who had come for her funeral. "Is Grandmother in heaven now?" Mehul asked his mother.

Mehul's mother was fixing food to serve after the church services were over. She was tired after their long trip and distracted about the arrangements. "Your grandmother was a good woman," she said as she sliced some bread. "I am sure she is in heaven."

"Can she see angels?" Mehul asked. Lately, he had become very interested in angels.

Mehul's mother put down the knife. "Mehul," she said quietly, "I think it would be a good idea for you to go next door to the church and say a prayer for Grandmother before everyone else gets there. Maybe it would help you to calm down."

Mehul thought he was calm enough already. But he knew his mother was sad, so he went outside and down the path to the quiet little brick church that he and his family attended when they visited India. He decided to sit in the familiar surroundings and think about his grandmother. Better still, he would ask the angels to find her in heaven, to show her around and take special care of her, because she was new there.

Mehul opened the church door and walked in. Then he stopped, horrified. The church was ruined!

"Oh, no!" Mehul could hardly believe his eyes. Broken candles lay scattered across the floor. Someone had written swear words on the walls in dark letters. Things on the altar were knocked over, and the cross was split in half.

Mehul stared in dismay. Why would anyone do such a thing, especially to a church? Especially when a funeral would start very soon. It made him sick just to look at the mess. How could his family say good-bye to Grandmother in the middle of this?

He turned and ran the short distance home. "Mama!" he shouted, bursting into the kitchen. "Someone has wrecked the church! There are plants overturned, candles broken!"

One of Mehul's aunts had just arrived. "Vandals must have done it!" she cried. "There have been several public buildings damaged recently. Oh, what will we do?"

Mehul's mother threw her apron onto the table. "Show me, son," she said, following Mehul out the door.

Seconds later, Mehul pushed open the church door. "Look, Mama!" he cried.

Mehul's mother stopped. "Look at what?"

Mehul stared in astonishment, blinked, and stared again. He could hardly believe his eyes. The church was in perfect order. Wax candles stood straight and tall and unbroken in their polished brass holders. The cross was mended and back on the wall. No bad words marred the smoothness of the walls. All the debris was gone.

"Mehul, how could this be?" his mother demanded. "If there was a mess here—"

"There was a mess!" Mehul declared. "I saw it!"

"Then who could have cleaned it up, in just a few moments?"

No one, Mehul admitted. Well, no one except a heavenly cleaning crew.

A warm feeling came over Mehul. He could almost see the glow of halos reflecting off the shiny candlesticks, for hadn't he just been talking to the angels, asking them to take care of things?

He knew that they were watching over Grandmother—and his whole family.

Song from Another Time

Think; in mounting higher.
The angels would press on us, and aspire
To drop some golden orb of perfect song
Into our deep dear silence.

—ELIZABETH BARRETT BROWNING

Six-year-old Janet had always had a certain memory, something she couldn't quite get hold of, like a little wisp of smoke. Her memory involved a sunny, wonderful place where she had been before she came to the earth. She remembered joyful sounds. Once or twice Janet had tried to describe to people this vague memory, but they thought it might have been a dream or a recollection from when she was a baby. Maybe they were right.

One night, Janet was sent to her room because she had been arguing with her sister. "It's almost bedtime, sweetheart," her mother said, "so put on your pajamas and say your night prayers. Ask God to help you have a happier day tomorrow."

Janet undressed slowly, feeling a little sad. She knew her mother was disappointed in her. Was God? She got on her knees. "Well, God," she began, "I haven't been very good today."

Just then she heard a sound. It sounded like people singing, far away. As she listened intently, the voices grew louder, closer. Was a video playing nearby? No, the whole family was downstairs. Janet could hear her older sisters teasing one another as they did the supper dishes. Bewildered, she got up, looked around her room, then went to check the outside hallway, just in case. Oddly, when she left her room, the music stopped.

Quickly, Janet returned, knelt down, and resumed her prayers. And the singing started again!

Janet listened intently. She didn't recognize the song, and she couldn't hear any instruments. But for some reason, she felt she had heard this choir before. The concert was rich and full and beautiful, as if a vast crowd were rejoicing. The song made her heart swell and tears come to her eyes.

Suddenly, she knew: they were angels! And they had sung that way to her, long ago in a warm and loving place, when she had no remembrance of anything but light and beauty.

The harmonies made her feel so joyful, as if God were giving her a tender hug. Janet knew that God wasn't disappointed in her at all.

For the next few years, Janet heard music whenever she prayed alone in her room. And she'd pray as long as she could so the glorious melody wouldn't stop. "I thought this happened to everyone," she says today. "Perhaps angels sing all of us to earth, but most of us just don't remember."

She didn't tell anyone, thinking that people would laugh. Until the singing episodes ended when she was about eleven, they remained a secret between her and the angels, who had reminded her just how much she and every person is loved.

Why don't all of us hear heavenly music, as Janet did? Who knows? God's ways are not our ways. But God has given us a precious promise, that God will send angels to guard us in all our ways (Psalm 91), and for that we can all rejoice!

DIANE'S DECISION

In the world you will have trouble, but take courage,
I have conquered the world.
—JOHN 16:33

Although angels are all around us, they don't always act to save us. Bad things often do happen to good people. We often don't understand why, but God does have a plan for each of us, and God can help us bring happiness out of suffering, not only for ourselves but also for others.

One evening, nine-year-old Diane; her thirteen-year-old sister, Gloria; and her eleven-year-old brother, David, were walking home from church in their neighborhood in Pittsburgh, Pennsylvania. Diane's mother had a chronic illness and never missed a chance to pray for herself or her family. Now, as she and the three children approached the neighborhood grocery store, she decided to pick up a few items. The children settled themselves outside on the shopping cart gate to wait for Mom. They'd done it hundreds of times.

"I remember how incredible the stars were," Diane says, "and everything seemed so peaceful. There were two little black girls also waiting." Diane and one of the girls exchanged smiles. Somehow she seemed familiar, yet Diane didn't think any of them had ever met. "The five of us started singing songs together, and it just seemed like we'd known each other forever."

The children were midway through a rousing chorus of "You Are My Sunshine" when their serene surroundings were shattered. "Look out!" one of the girls shouted. A car was racing through the parking lot directly toward them. Diane panicked and looked around. Shopping carts were blocking them from running—so to get away, she jumped into a cart. She intended to use it as a shield, but one of her legs got caught in the seat. At fifty miles per hour, the drunk driver crashed into the group of terrified children. The next thing Diane remembers is sitting on the sidewalk, looking at herself and screaming. Her left leg below the knee had been torn away.

"I saw my sister, Gloria, lying to my right, not moving but making moaning sounds," Diane says. "My brother was murmuring something. The two little girls were nowhere in sight. I wondered if they had been killed because there was nowhere for them to have run." People raced out of the store, and Diane's mother began to scream as she surveyed the scene. Oddly, an ambulance had pulled up right after the car had crashed through the lot. The off-duty paramedic, they later discovered, had stopped to buy cigarettes, something he rarely did. But because of his kind and professional presence, the children all arrived at the hospital within ten minutes and lived, despite the loss of blood. The doctors, of course, could do nothing about Diane's missing limb. For the rest of her life, she would wear an artificial left leg.

As word of the tragedy spread throughout the hospital on that first terrible night, an African American man sought out Diane's father. "I'd like to donate my blood for your daughters," he said.

In the midst of his terror, Diane's father agreed. The stranger did so, stayed the rest of the night with Diane's parents, and later showed up at some of the court hearings to lend moral support. Diane never had a chance to meet him and was surprised later when there didn't seem to be any information available about him. It was odd, Diane thought, that although the vast majority of their friends were white and would later step up willingly to help the family, the first person to offer help was black, with no apparent connection to them. But at that point, the family was in shock, traumatized by a drunk driver who had lost control of his car and changed their world forever.

"The next morning, I woke up feeling calm and cheerful," Diane says. "My parents were at my bedside crying, but I told them not to be sad because I was alive, and that's what mattered." Even when Diane confirmed that her left leg was gone, she merely shrugged and said, "Well, that's too bad." She was in shock, everyone thought.

But, despite the trauma and the pain, Diane remained serene. "I'm not sure why I was able to be so positive about it at such a young age," she says, "but I always knew I had some special beings up there helping me through life."

Diane was in the hospital off and on for about a year and had frequent operations to repair the damage caused by the loss of her leg. The doctors tried hard to restore part of it with skin grafts and bone reconstruction so she could success-fully wear an artificial leg. The surgeries were painful and not always successful. The hospital chaplain would give her the last rites whenever she went into surgery. "I didn't understand that I was in danger of death due to all the anesthesia," she says. "I just thought he was being nice to me!"

Her upbeat attitude continued even after she went home to a hospital bed in the living room of their small house, a cast on her remaining leg. "My mother wore a hearing aid, and at night she would take it out and sleep on the couch near me, in case I needed the bedpan or something." One night Diane's mother was awakened by something. When she looked over at Diane, she saw an African American woman standing beside her sleeping daughter. "The woman had her hand on me, and she was dressed all in white, and she turned and looked at my mother and smiled," Diane says. "My mother blinked to see if she was real, and the woman disappeared."

Diane had also been thinking about the two little girls at the accident scene. No one had mentioned them, and they had obviously not been injured. Had they been angels? If so, could they have been trying to protect Diane's family from the drunk driver, but weren't able to do so? Did angels appear in different races, for different reasons? It seemed logical to her.

Perhaps this heavenly connection was why Diane never seemed depressed about her situation. "It would take more than the loss of a leg to get me down," she says. "I love life." When she was thirteen, she even phoned the driver who had hit her and told him she had forgiven him. He was stunned at her openness. "I will never understand what could make a person get that drunk and then drive, but I felt that I needed to contact him," she says. Her attitude eventually rubbed off on her sister Gloria as well (who was also badly hurt in the accident), and both sisters developed the courage and forgiving attitude that has made life such a gift.

Her doctors doubted that she would heal extensively, but Diane surprised everyone. She received her prosthesis at age fifteen and hasn't slowed down since. Today she is married to her high-school sweetheart and handles a blended family of five children. "I believe there is a reason God didn't take me and my brother and sister to his home that night," she says, "and I'm excited to find out what it is. Maybe I was meant to encourage others to not give up hope and to remember that God loves us all."

Why didn't God and the angels save Diane from this trauma rather than allowing her to go through it? We'll never know. But Diane made a choice to be happy in her circumstances, and she lights everyone's path with her attitude and faith. Thank you, Diane.

INVISIBLE ANGELS

Ever felt an angel's breath in the gentle breeze? A teardrop in the falling
rain? Hear a whisper amongst the rustle of leaves? Or been kissed by a
lone snowflake? Nature is an angel's favorite hiding place.
—CARRIE LATET

Ira was attending summer camp in the Catskill Mountains.
He knew he should be grateful that he could spend some
time in this beautiful area. Instead, he felt uncomfortable,
because he just didn't fit in with the other boys. They traveled
in loud, intimidating gangs and made everything an aggressive
contest. Ira was shy, and he longed for just one or two pals
who would share his interests and accept him.

One evening, feeling especially lonely, Ira walked away
from the dining hall and watched the sun slip toward the hori-
zon. How he wished he wasn't so quiet and reserved. But how

could he be anything else but the way God had made him? Ira was confused. *God, where are you?*

He had been walking for some time, down a path into the woods. He stopped near the edge of the lake. The sun was gently setting, leaving pink and golden trails in the blue sky. Ira could hear nothing but a few birds chirping and the lapping of water against the shore. He sat on a large branch and took his siddur, a Jewish prayer book, out of his pocket. Slowly, he read the familiar Hebrew words. Oh, if only he knew God was listening to him. "God, are you there?" he asked aloud.

Suddenly, the woods began to rumble. Ira looked up in alarm. The trees above him were wildly waving, swaying—as if they were signaling to him. Was a storm coming? No, the sky was still hazy and cloudless.

Ira stared at the billowing branches, and all of a sudden, everything stopped. A deep hush fell over the woods. Each tree seemed to hold its breath.

"God," Ira said aloud. "Was that you? Tell me if you're near me. I really need to know!"

Once more the air seemed electric, filled with activity. Although Ira felt no breeze, above him the trees again exploded in frenzied motion, as if angels were moving them in wide impossible arcs. The limbs bent to the ground in a bow. Underneath, the earth thundered and shook as if the trees were having a party, with people and angels smiling, laughing, and waving to him from heaven. And then again there was silence.

Ira's sadness and uncertainty dropped from him like a heavy cloak, and his heart grew warm with love—and relief. For he knew that God and the angels had just passed by and had left him with a special message of hope.

Miracles on the Way

*Miracles are not contrary to nature, but only contrary
to what we know about nature.*
—St. Augustine

Rachel had loved playing the clarinet ever since the fourth grade, and now she was in the high school marching band. It had been hard learning to play and march at the same time; in the beginning Rachel had taken many wrong turns and walked right into other members of the band! But it was already October, and with several performances at football games behind her, she was feeling like a pro.

The band had played a good half-time program, and the game was almost over. "Going to the party tonight?" asked Rachel's friend Jackie, as she came up behind her in the band room.

"Uh-huh," Rachel answered. She hurriedly put her clarinet in its case and turned toward the door. "But I've got to get home to shower and change first."

"Want a ride?" Jackie asked. "My mom will be here in a few minutes."

Rachel hesitated. It was already dark. But sometimes Jackie's mom was late, and Rachel wanted to be at the party by nine. Besides, Rachel loved to run. People up and down her street had seen her streak by ever since she was a little kid. "There goes Rachel," they would say to one another. "Have you ever seen any child run so fast?"

It had been awhile since she had had a long satisfying sprint. "Thanks, but I think I'll run home," she told Jackie. "See you at the party!"

Rachel warmed up quickly, took off, and dashed past the football field. The game had just ended, and fans were spilling onto the quiet avenues that surrounded the high school. She passed most of them in no time, heading down the street. She wasn't even breathing hard yet. The crowd was thinning out, so Rachel put on some speed, dashing diagonally across Ninth

Street and up a hill. It was great to be running, to have her hair streaming out behind her, to be feeling free and happy.

Bam! Rachel slammed into what felt like a wall. The impact was so hard that she bounced back, staggered, and landed on her knees. A woman jogging behind her saw her fall. "Are you all right?" she called.

What had she hit? Somewhat stunned and breathless, Rachel looked for a barricade blocking her path. But there was nothing there! She had collided with a huge, invisible something.

Just then a car full of teenagers roared over the hill and past her, so close that she could feel the ground beneath her shake, the wind strong on her cheeks. She hadn't even heard anything coming. Had she not run into the invisible obstacle, she would have been in the middle of the street, right in the automobile's path. The car never could have stopped in time.

"What a close call!" The woman behind her came running up. "How fortunate that you tripped!"

Rachel got up, examining the holes in the knees of her band uniform. She hadn't tripped, but she knew the woman would never believe her.

She put out her hand. As silently as it had come, the protective barrier had vanished. Nothing was blocking her way. But something had, just in time. And Rachel knew who it was. "Thank you, guardian angel," she whispered as she jogged slowly on to her house.

Tynan Barnes, of Garland, Texas, had come home during his class break to gather his baseball gear. A senior in high school, Tynan was on the baseball team, and an away game was planned for after school. Tynan grabbed his equipment, jumped back into his 1967 red Mustang, and sped back to school. Twenty minutes later, as his mother, Janet, was leaving for a dental appointment, she heard sirens. Cautiously she drove to the main street in her neighborhood and looked to her left. At the corner of the block down the street, there had been an accident. Janet's heart almost stopped—the car involved was red, similar to Tynan's Mustang. "I denied my sinking stomach and turned right," Janet says, "But I only got a short distance. My spirit was telling me to go back and check out the car."

Janet made a U-turn and drove toward the wreck. A police officer waved at her to go on her way, but she stopped for a moment. "Officer, this car may be my son's." Immediately, the officer helped her out. She was glad of his strength, because the closer they got to the car, the more positive she was that it was Tynan's.

But where was Tynan? Buried under the mass of steel? Janet saw that there was another vehicle involved, a pickup truck. "Your son is in an ambulance on his way to the emergency room," the officer told Janet. He had been calling the school, trying to discover her or her husband's phone numbers, when she drove up. "What happened?" Janet asked him, hardly believing the terrible twisted metal all around her.

"Your son stopped at the intersection stop sign," the officer explained. "Then he started on and was broadsided by a small pickup truck that ran the sign. If he hadn't been wearing his seat belt . . ." The officer shook his head. "He was shoved over to the passenger side, and without the belt he would have flown right out the passenger window. Ma'am, he would have died right here."

Thank you, God. But how was Tynan now? Had he survived the ambulance ride? Janet raced to the emergency room, where, finally, she was able to speak to the doctors. "You're lucky he was driving a heavy car," one doctor said, "and especially that he was wearing his seat belt. Otherwise he would have gone out the window." Other personnel agreed. The seatbelt had saved their son's life.

Janet and her husband finally found Tynan, battered and in pain but blessedly alive. He was talking to the hospital personnel and had not yet been given any painkillers. But something miraculous had happened to him, and he was trying to explain it.

At the scene, Tynan said, he had opened his eyes and seen a glorious looking sky and ground, all brilliantly white and beautiful. He was in heaven! "There was no central source of light like we have with the sun," he says, "but the light came from everywhere." Tynan started to see people he loved and cared for. Wonder filled him, and as he turned to see more, he heard God. "It is not your time yet."

"He said it with so much love and authority that I felt as though I was in a kingdom filled with love," Tynan says. As soon as God spoke, Tynan found himself back in his car.

Now in the hospital, Tynan tried to describe what had happened. "I saw God, Mom," he whispered. "He told me I'd be fine."

Janet had a tingly feeling. "You're going to be fine, Tynan." She touched his cheek. "Because you did the right thing. You had your seat belt on, and I'm so glad."

"But Mom," Tynan murmured. "I didn't."

"You must have. You always do. Everyone here is saying that the seat belt saved your life."

Tynan looked puzzled. "I was in a hurry—I had to get back to school to make the bus for the game, and I just never put it on."

Then Janet knew what had happened. "God must have told the angels to buckle Tynan up," she says, "and then to release him to the paramedics' care. It's the only way he could have survived."

Tynan spent eight weeks in the hospital and even celebrated his eighteenth birthday there. His injuries included a pelvic bone broken in three places, a lacerated spleen, four broken ribs, collapsed lungs, and a torn-up thumb; yet he recovered beautifully and today is the father of a young family.

Even though Tynan had forgotten his safety rules, God saved him anyway. Do you think we always have to be doing the "right" thing for God to love us and take care of us?

From the Depths

Life comes packaged in light and dark.
—Antoinette Bosco

Ten-year-old Betsy was spending the day at a beach in Southern California with her mom, her brothers, and her little sister. As the children stood knee-deep in the swirling surf, their mother warned them about the undertow. "Don't go too far out," she cautioned. "You may think you can swim back to shore, but sometimes people get carried away by the tide and drown."

Betsy could feel the strong pull of the current on her legs, and for a while she played carefully near the shore. Gradually, however, she paddled farther from where Mom lay on the blanket, reading her book. Betsy was having so much fun that she didn't realize how far out she had gone. Then she turned around to go back to shore.

She couldn't! The current was pulling her out to sea!

"Oh, no!" Betsy swam as fast as she could, but her efforts were useless against the water's powerful push. "Mommy, help!" she screamed, and she started to cry. But no one was near her, and no one heard. The beach seemed so far away that the people looked like little toys. Exhausted and terrified, Betsy felt herself sinking. The sky slowly disappeared, and everything started to get dark.

She was under the surface of the water! Betsy prayed out loud. "God, please help me." She could hear her own words clearly, yet no water entered her mouth. Everything around her started to get brighter, almost as if the water itself were made of light. What was happening? Was this what it felt like to drown? If so, instead of being frightened, Betsy felt a soft peace stealing over her. It was strange, but somehow she knew that God was very close.

Just then Betsy felt a strong hand gripping her wrist. Someone was pulling her firmly up, up, up, with such incredible speed that she felt almost weightless. She broke through the waves and somehow found herself sitting on the back of a surfboard, holding tightly to a teenage boy. "Oh, thank you for saving me!" Betsy gasped.

"What are you talking about?" The boy looked back at her with a bewildered expression.

"Didn't you grab me just now?" Betsy asked.

"No," the surfer answered. "I was riding a wave—my last one of the day. I was approaching the shore, and then . . ." He shook his head. "Now I'm sitting on my board, back where I started, and you're here. Who are you? And where did you come from?"

As he paddled toward shore, Betsy explained what had happened to her. "How could this be?" the boy asked. "I didn't pull you—in fact, I didn't see you at all until you landed on my board behind me."

How had the boy suddenly gotten from shore to the place out in the surf where Betsy was? Who had gripped her, pulled her up, and placed her safely on the surfboard? In fact, how had she been able to call out to God from under the surface of the water and not get water in her lungs?

By the time Betsy reached the shore, she was as dumb-founded as her rescuer. But there was one more surprise in store for her. "Mom, did you see what happened to me?" Betsy made her way to the blanket.

"Yes, dear, I saw you swim in. Are you having fun?" Mom asked, smiling.

Swim in? But Betsy had ridden on the back of a surfboard. She turned around, but her rescuer had disappeared.

Perhaps he was just an ordinary boy; he certainly had seemed as confused as she. But if that were so, why hadn't Betsy's mother seen him, too? And surely no ordinary boy could have found her so precisely under the waves or pulled her to the surface with such speed and strength.

For years, Betsy told no one about her adventure in the water. "God was holding on to me that day to let me know that God was real and the only One who could save me," she says. For a long time, it was a moment too special to share.

A Message for Joanie

Perhaps they are not stars but rather openings in heaven, where the love of our lost ones pours through and shines down upon us, to let us know they are happy.

—An Eskimo legend

Joanie, wake up!"

Joanie yawned and rolled over, her eyes still shut tightly. It couldn't be morning yet. She felt as though she had just fallen asleep.

But there was that insistent hand on her shoulder again, shaking her into awareness. "Joanie, you have to get up!"

"Mom?" Slowly, Joanie opened her eyes and saw her mother's distraught face over her. It was the middle of the night. What was happening?

"Joanie, I can't take time to explain." Mom was guiding her gently out of bed, putting on her bathrobe for her as if she were a baby. "But Dad and I have to leave, and you need to stay awake and listen for the children. They'd be frightened if they woke up, and Dad and I weren't here."

Eleven-year-old Joanie was the oldest of five, and her mother sometimes called her "my extra pair of hands"! Their family was very close, and Mom and Dad hardly ever did anything without explaining. This middle-of-the-night event was very odd.

"Are you awake now?" Mom was leading Joanie downstairs. In the light of the hallway she could see her father hurriedly putting on his overcoat. He gave her a worried smile.

"I'm awake, Mom, but what's happening?"

"We can't talk now, dear. We'll be back as soon as we can." Her mother grabbed her purse and followed Daddy out the door. Joanie heard their car speeding away, the sound of its engine loud in the deserted street.

What could have happened? Joanie went into the living room, slumped in a comfortable chair, and turned on the table lamp. Its rays shone on the hall clock. It was 4 a.m. Joanie couldn't remember ever being up at this time. How was she going to stay awake until dawn?

And then it seemed as if she was no longer alone in the room. She felt a presence, something warm and wonderful. Joanie was not at all afraid. *Is someone there?* she asked silently.

Do not be worried, the presence answered. *God has just taken your grandmother to heaven, and now she is with him.*

Grandma had died! Now Joanie realized why her parents had seemed so worried and had been in such a hurry. No wonder they had not told Joanie what was happening. They didn't want to leave her to grieve all by herself.

But she wasn't grieving. She loved Grandma very much, and she knew she ought to feel sad. But there seemed to be an air of happiness, even bliss, in the living room.

That soothing, wonderful voice had seemed to be male. Now Joanie heard another voice, a woman's voice. It was Grandma! "I am all right, Joanie," Grandma said out loud. "Everyone will be very sad, but you must be strong and tell them that I am all right, and that I'm in heaven now."

Your grandmother was so loved, and now she is very happy, the first voice added. *She has done all she can to be ready for this special day.*

Joanie was awestruck. Was she having a dream? No, she knew her grandmother's voice. And the other voice—it was hard to tell whether it was coming from outside or whether it was speaking inside her, to her heart. But she knew—without knowing how she knew—that it was the voice of Grandma's guardian angel.

Then, unbelievably, Grandma was standing in front of her! She looked just like she did in a black-and-white portrait of herself and Grandpa that had always hung in their bedroom. Was this a picture, too? No, Grandma was moving, smiling—she looked beautiful! She had always been a happy woman and now she seemed radiant with joy.

"Oh, Grandma, I love you. I'm going to miss you so much!" Joanie's eyes filled with tears. But they were not tears of sorrow. There was too much warmth, love, and hope in the room for her to be sad.

"Joanie, don't worry," Grandma reminded her again. "Tell everyone I'm happy."

Then time seemed to stand still, and the living room was bathed in a luminous glow. Joanie basked in the presence of Grandma and her unseen guardian. She didn't need to talk. Just being in this special place, with these special beings, was enough.

Gradually, the images faded, and Joanie fell asleep for awhile. The next sound she heard was her baby brother stirring upstairs. Six a.m. It was time to see about getting breakfast.

A few hours later, Joanie's father came home. "We have some bad news," he said, drawing her aside. "Your grandmother has died. We were racing to meet the ambulance at the hospital after Grandpa phoned us, but we didn't get there in time to talk to her. It happened very suddenly."

"What time did Grandma die?" Joanie asked.

"Just at four o'clock," Daddy answered.

Joanie thought of her marvelous encounter in the living room, at 4 a.m. "Daddy, we don't need to be sad," she said. "Grandma's already in heaven. She's happier than she's ever been. She told me to tell you this."

No one paid much attention to Joanie in the days that followed. Everyone seemed steeped in grief. But although Joanie had loved her grandmother very much, she felt no sorrow at all. Grandma was safe with God and the angels, and she had come to tell her so.

THE TOUCH OF LOVE

*Rows of angels stood on either side, their large wings arched high
above their heads, waving to me like I was their friend.
"Welcome, Kyle!" they said.*
—KYLE WOODARD, *ONE OF THE CROWD*

L ora was the kind of girl who just couldn't sit still.

"Calm down, Lora!" her mother always told her.

"Why can't you settle down and concentrate!" her teachers
complained.

Lora didn't know why it was so hard for her to be quiet
and learn, as the other kids in her second-grade class did. And
she wondered why everyone else could figure out the words
and numbers on the pages so easily. To her, the words often
looked like mysterious squiggly lines.

Sometimes Lora tried very hard to behave. When she caught her knee bouncing or her pencil tapping, she'd tell every part of her to cut it out! But a few minutes later, her knee would be bouncing or her pencil tapping again.

At other times, though, Lora just didn't care. If people didn't like her the way she was, she couldn't help it—and she wouldn't try to change their minds. But inside, it still hurt. At night she would lie awake, praying, "God, please make tomorrow better. Please let me pay attention and be a good girl." But nothing ever seemed to change. The next day would be the same as the one before, with Lora getting into trouble again.

One morning Lora was having an especially hard time sitting still. "Lora!" her teacher asked. "Have you finished your workbook papers?"

Lora looked at the papers. Squiggly lines. Strange marks. She couldn't figure them out.

"No," she said quietly. The boy sitting across from her stared at her. The girl behind her started to giggle.

"Lora, come up to my desk, please," the teacher said.

Lora stood up. Everyone in the class was watching her, and she felt as though she would be sick. Holding her chin up, she walked to the front of the room.

"I want you to go and sit in the library by yourself for a while," the teacher told her. "Perhaps when you come back, you'll decide to complete your assignments as the other children are doing."

Lora slowly left the classroom and walked down the hall. Her cheeks were hot with shame, and her stomach felt even sicker. Deep in her throat she felt a burning sensation, and she wanted to cry.

She slumped down in a chair in the empty library. What was wrong with her? Why couldn't she learn like the other kids? Being sent to the library was a punishment, and it had already happened to her several times this year. It never helped; when she went back to class, her knee still bounced and the lines in the books still seemed to move. When her parents found out about the punishment, her mother would be mad, and her father, too—although Lora knew they were more worried than angry over her behavior.

What was she going to do? She was stupid and ugly—no wonder everyone laughed at her. Lora put her head down on her arms and let the tears come.

She thought she was alone in the library. But she felt a hand on her shoulder, a peaceful hand. It was patting her on the shoulder, caressing her in the nicest way, somehow making her feel a great sense of love in every part of her. Then a voice spoke right behind her. It didn't sound like a man or a woman, but it was the kindest voice she had ever heard. "Don't worry, little Lora," it said gently. "Everything is going to be all right."

Slowly, a feeling of comfort seeped into Lora's heart. She felt as if the person behind her knew all about her and loved her anyway. Who was it? She lifted her tearful face and turned around.

But there was no one there. No one in the library at all, except two older girls studying together on the other side of the room.

Lora could still feel the imprint of the warm supportive hand on her shoulder, still hear the sound of the voice soothing her raw spirit. "Don't worry, little Lora. Don't worry."

Life wasn't the same for Lora after that. The following year, her third-grade teacher discovered that Lora had learning disabilities, and she taught Lora to do her schoolwork in new ways. Relieved that Lora's problems had answers, that she hadn't been misbehaving on purpose, Lora's parents made an extra effort to encourage her.

And when she still occasionally had trouble quieting down, Lora would remember the calming voice, the reassurance of that special day. She knew that an angel had come to tell her that—squiggly lines or straight, wiggly or still—she was loved.

WINGED WARRIORS

Lord, keep us safe this night
Secure from all our fears.
May angels guard us while we sleep,
Till morning light appears. Amen.

—TRADITIONAL ANGEL PRAYER

Juan and Danny's parents were divorced, and the boys were getting ready to spend Saturday with Dad, as they did every week. Dad's apartment was being painted, so tonight they would be staying overnight in the apartment of his new girlfriend, Marguerite.

"Bye, Mom." Ten-year-old Juan gave his mother a big hug. Danny, age eight, did the same. The boys wished their parents were still together, but spending special time with their dad was the next best thing.

"Behave yourself." Mom smiled at them.

"We will."

It was a good day. They went with Dad and his girlfriend to the park, where they played baseball and grilled hamburgers. Finally, after they'd had their baths and watched some television, Dad tucked them into Marguerite's king-sized bed. "Marguerite and I are going outside for a walk," Daddy assured them. "You go to sleep now."

The bed was roomy and comfortable, and Juan felt himself drifting off to sleep right away. Suddenly, however, Danny poked him. "Juan! Juan!" Danny whispered. He sounded frightened.

"What?"

"The ceiling! Look at the ceiling!"

Juan looked up. He couldn't see anything in the dark room. "What are you talking about?"

"Can't you see the scary faces up there? They look like monsters, and they're staring at me."

Juan rolled over and closed his eyes. "Danny, you're just dreaming, that's all. Go to sleep. There's no such thing as monsters."

A few moments passed, then Danny poked Juan again. "They're still there! See them? Juan, they're so ugly! I'm scared."

Juan sighed. At this rate, he'd be up all night. "Danny, go back to sleep," he murmured. "It's all in your mind."

Another moment passed. Juan could hear Danny crying quietly. He rolled over again. "Danny, I'm getting mad!"

"Juan, you have to do something!" Juan's eyes had gotten used to the darkness, and he could see Danny staring at the ceiling, wide-eyed with terror. Juan looked up again.

At first he didn't see anything but the ceiling. But, what was that? Juan saw a dim face, then another face, until the whole ceiling seemed to be filled with them. Danny was right—they were hideous, evil, and they looked like the pictures of devils that he had seen in books!

The faces were not moving. They seemed to be painted on the ceiling, like a mural. And yet, oddly, the scenes kept shifting again and again, showing more creatures with different expressions and poses. It was as if he were looking at a terrifying slide show.

Juan turned away from the faces. He must be dreaming. He had to be dreaming! But he knew this was real.

He should grab Danny right now, jump out of bed, and escape from the room. But what if there were more evil beings in the living room? The boys had never been in this apartment before. What if something was terribly wrong with it?

Danny was still crying beside him. "I want Mommy," he sobbed.

Juan wanted her, too. And then he remembered something. "Whenever you are frightened," his mother always told them, "just ask God to send the angels to protect you."

They could do that. Even with devils looking at them from the ceiling, they could pray. Juan reached for Danny's hand and held it tightly. "Let's ask the angels to come," he said.

They didn't know quite how to ask, but special words didn't seem to be necessary. "Angels, help us," both boys murmured again and again. And as they prayed, the ceiling began to change. The ugly faces had been on a black background, but as Juan watched intently, the ceiling faded into white. Then an angel appeared at the right corner, a large winged warrior! "Do you see it, Danny?" Juan whispered, excited.

"Yes! It's an angel!" Danny answered. "And look, there's another, and another!"

Enthralled, both boys watched as big, strong angels began to fill the air above them, again not moving, but as scenes shifting, one after another. Each scene brought more and more angels, moving from right to left across the ceiling, pushing the ugly faces to the edges of the room. *They are fighting for us*, Juan realized in awe. He knew that he was seeing something most people never glimpse: the invisible battles of the spirit world.

Slowly, slowly, the devils gave way, until only angels remained, wonderful beings who not only filled the ceiling but also came down the walls, surrounding the boys with protection. Cozy and warm, the two fell into blissful sleep.

When Juan and Daniel came home on Sunday, they told their mother what had happened. She did not laugh at them. Instead, she did some checking. Why had they been so terrified? What had been going on in Marguerite's apartment?

Eventually, she learned that Marguerite and some of her friends had been using the apartment for occult activities. These women had invited evil spirits into their lives, and undoubtedly Juan and Danny had felt their presence when they stayed overnight.

Obviously, God doesn't want anyone getting involved in things that are frightening. It's smart to avoid not only violent video games and movies but also Ouija boards, tarot cards, fortune-telling, and books about witchcraft. People sometimes assume that such things are only games, but they can also be doorways to danger from the dark side of the spirit world.

Fortunately, the boys had known what to do. "I still feel angels around me today," Juan says. "I know that, whatever happens, we can call on them for help."

A Cradle of Love

For He will command His angels to guard you in all
your ways;
They will lift you up in their hands, so that you will not
strike your foot against a stone.
—PSALM 92:11–12

Eight-year-old Daniel lived in Buenos Aires, Argentina. In the big city, the architecture is very mixed, with high apartment buildings, like towers, next to two-story buildings, and low houses all around. Today was the day Daniel was going to attend his friend José's birthday party.

José lived just two blocks away from Daniel. The two always walked to school together, and Daniel had often played on the big terrace behind José's house. From the terrace, the boys could see the roofs of surrounding houses. A wall separated them from the building next door.

That afternoon, Daniel walked to José's house, carrying a birthday present for him. Several boys were already on the terrace. "Hey, Daniel!" one shouted. "You're just in time to play ball."

Daniel joined his pals, and the boys threw the ball around. All of a sudden someone missed a catch, and the ball sailed over the wall onto the roof of the building next door. Instantly, the boys climbed up the wall and scrambled onto the roof.

"There's the ball!" Daniel saw it first, lying on top of a glass skylight. Daniel had seen such skylights before, on top of his school's roof. Daniel knew the glass in skylights was thick and hard. This large pane would hold him easily. Daniel stepped up onto the skylight and reached for the ball.

Crash! The window shattered into a million pieces. Daniel fell through it and hurtled toward the floor below.

His fall seemed to take hours. Feeling as if he were in slow motion, Daniel spun upside down and around, completely out of control. Finally, he landed.

Although he had fallen more than two stories, he seemed to be fine. Daniel gingerly felt his head, arms, and legs. Nothing was broken. He sat up. In spite of all the jagged glass surrounding him, he could see only one small cut on his right arm. It didn't even hurt. Nothing hurt.

"Daniel? Are you all right?" His panic-stricken friends were shouting down from the top of the roof near the skylight. José, they said, had run to his house to get help.

"I think so," he called back. He slowly got to his feet, grateful but confused. Soon he heard a key turn in a door, and José's parents came running in to find him.

José's mother gave him a big hug. "The people who live in this house are on vacation," she explained. "They left their key with us."

José's father was looking around. "Daniel must have landed on this chair," he said. "That's what broke his fall."

Daniel turned around. There was an old, ugly armchair behind him, tilting because of a broken leg. Now he remembered; he had landed on it before hitting the floor.

But something was very odd. Daniel realized that he was in a luxurious living room, beautifully furnished. Why would such an old chair be in a room like this? Especially right underneath a skylight, as if it had been placed there just for him?

No one, not even the owners of the house, ever discovered who owned the chair or where it had come from. "I thought it was a great coincidence at first," Daniel says. "But I believe my guardian angel moved that chair from somewhere else, to save my life. He was watching out for me that day. And he still does."

"Lisa! Come out and skate with us!" Fifth grader Lisa looked out her window. Her two best friends, Janice and Karen, were skating up and down the sidewalk in front of Lisa's house and calling to her. It didn't take Lisa long to grab her in-line skates and cruise out to join them.

In summer, the girls skated every day. It was, by far, the most fun thing to do. They had to be careful, of course, especially when they built up speed, because the sidewalks in their neighborhood were old, with bumpy and uneven places. Tripping over a broken piece of concrete could cause a bad fall.

But that never slowed them down. "Let's race!" Janice shouted, and all three started off down the sidewalk. Lisa's long hair streamed out behind her as she built up speed. Soon she was laughing out loud.

And she was winning their contest by at least three house-widths! Lisa looked behind her and grinned at her friends. Just then she felt her back foot hit a large crack in the sidewalk.

Lisa was skating so fast that she flew into the air, her feet in front of her. Then she began to fall backward. She was going to land right on the top of her head, and there was nothing she could do! "Lisa!" her friends screamed behind her.

Lisa's long hair was already touching the sidewalk, and she braced herself for the impact and the pain.

Then she felt the pressure of two hands at the top of her back. Big hands, steady hands—they were pushing her back up onto her feet. Suddenly she was upright though shaky. And then those hands gave her another push, this time a gentle one, and she fell forward into the soft grass.

Janice and Karen glided up, breathless and astounded. "How did you do that?" Janice asked. "You were falling upside down, and then you stood right side up again!"

Lisa hesitated, then told her friends about those wonderful, invisible hands.

The girls' eyes grew big. "Maybe it was an angel," Karen suggested.

That's what Lisa thought, too. What other answer could there be?

Ten-year-old Lee and his two brothers loved to play on the wooden stairs that connected the first floor of their house with the second. Sometimes they slid down the steep banister. Other times they jumped from the third—or fourth, or fifth—step to the floor below. And when their mother told them to bring down the laundry from the bedrooms so she could wash everyone's clothes, the boys would do it by dropping the clothes at the top of the stairs and sliding on them all the way down!

When playing, Lee had to be a little more careful than his brothers. His left foot turned inward, and from time to time he would lose his balance and stumble. "Tanglefoot!" his brothers occasionally teased when they saw his bumps and bruises. Lee didn't mind being teased, but falling on those bare wooden stairs really hurt, and he was always just a little afraid of that.

One morning his mother called to him from downstairs. "Lee, hurry up! You'll be late for school!"

"Coming!" Quickly, Lee rounded the corner and started down the stairs. Horrified, he felt himself slip. His feet went out from under him, and he somersaulted down, crashing against the wall, then the banister. Sure that he would break a bone or crack his head, Lee tried to grab the spokes in the banister to stop his wild tumbling, but he couldn't.

Then his skid seemed to stop, in midair. Lee felt as though he were cushioned in a cloud. He was tumbling down the last three steps now, but they weren't hard at all. In fact, he could hardly feel them.

Bounce, bounce, bounce. Gently, Lee floated to the floor, landing on what felt like a feather pillow, soft and fluffy.

Slowly, he stood up. He felt just fine. And there wasn't a mark on him. But there wasn't a pillow on the floor either. Everything looked just as it always did. How had Lee been so softly shielded? "I fell down the stairs," he told his mother who had just run to him, "but it felt like someone caught me."

His mother just smiled.

THE CHRISTMAS ANGEL

You are the bows from which your children as living arrows are sent forth.
—KHALIL GIBRAN, *THE PROPHET*

It was a few days before Christmas in Hamilton, Indiana. Kari had gone with her baby sister, Amy, and her mom on some errands, and they were buying a few things at the grocery store. Kari was a bit tired. She would rather have stayed at home, but her mom needed her to help watch Amy.

Finally, they unloaded their items at the checkout counter. Kari looked idly around, then noticed a plastic mayonnaise jar on a shelf near the cash register. A picture of a girl was taped on it, and below that was a handwritten sign that read, "Beth L has cancer, desperately needs donations for a bone marrow transplant."

Kari realized that she knew Beth, who was a couple of grades ahead of her in school. But Kari hadn't known Beth was sick.

"Look, Mom." Kari pointed at the empty jar. "I know this girl."

Her mother read the sign, and her eyes filled with tears. "That poor family—they must be so worried," she murmured.

"Could we give them some money?" Kari asked. Then she remembered with dismay how tight their own budget always was. There was no way Mom could spare anything, especially right now, just before Christmas.

Mom had just been handed several bills in change. She looked at the money for a moment, then put it all in the jar. "This is all I have," she said sadly. "I wish it were more."

Kari knew the donation was a real sacrifice. As they walked to the car, she felt tears start in her eyes. She was proud of what her mom had done.

Mom started the engine and pulled out of the parking lot. As the car headed down the dark highway, Kari closed her eyes tightly and prayed for Beth. What must it be like, having cancer and being scared?

Then Kari heard something hit the windshield. It sounded like a pebble. "Look at that!" her mother cried.

Kari's eyes popped open. A small ball of light, shining a bright silver blue, was bouncing on the outside of the front window. And then, unbelievably, it was inside the car, flashing and shining, getting bigger and bigger, wrapping them all in a brilliant cocoon.

Kari was astonished. The light couldn't be coming from outside; theirs was the only car on the dark road, and there were no streetlights along their route, not even any Christmas lights. Besides, the ball was far too bright to be a reflection. Awed, Kari watched it. It was dazzling, radiant, yet somehow joyful, too. It looked as if it were dancing. And was that the outline of a figure in its center? Kari couldn't tell for sure.

She looked outside and noticed that the whole area where they were riding seemed to be illuminated. She looked at Amy, whose eyes were wide in wonder.

As quickly as the light had appeared, it vanished, and the interior of the car was completely dark again. Kari's mother had pulled off the road, and she turned to Kari. "You look as shocked as I am," she said. "What did you see?"

"A ball of light! It came inside the car! Mom, what was it?"

"I don't know," her mother said thoughtfully. "Maybe it was a Christmas angel, bringing us a message of hope for Beth or thanking us for giving our money to her."

Kari thought about it. "Do angels do that? Do they bring good news to ordinary people like us?"

"They did on the first Christmas," her mother reminded her, smiling. "Why not now?" The strange light didn't return. But that Christmas turned out to be the best one Kari's family had ever had. Even though they didn't have much money, they felt very blessed, as if the joy of the bouncing light was still in their midst.

And when vacation ended, Kari received another gift. "How is Beth?" she asked a friend on their first day back in school.

"Oh, Beth had her transplant, and she's able to come back to school today."

Kari knew that not every sick person got well, especially not right away. Sometimes such things took time, because God's plan wasn't the same for everyone.

But no matter what the results seemed to be, God always wanted people to care for one another and to offer their help, even when it wasn't easy, even when it cost time or money. That was the best way to make earth more like heaven.

To make every day like Christmas.

NOTE FROM THE AUTHOR

I am always interested in sharing stories about angels and miracles. You can contact me at P.O. Box 127, Prospect Heights, IL 60070, or sign up to receive stories from my website, joanwanderson.com.